KU-491-263

Bruges and Ghent

Berlitz Publishing Company, Inc.
Princeton   Mexico City   Dublin   Eschborn   Singapore

Copyright © 1999 by Berlitz Publishing Co., Inc.
400 Alexander Park, Princeton, NJ, 08540 USA
9-13 Grosvenor St., London, W1X 9FB UK

All rights reserved. No part of this book may be reproduced or trans-
mitted in any form or by any means, electronic or mechanical, including photocopying, recording or by any information storage or
retrieval system without permission in writing from the publisher.

Berlitz Trademark Reg. U.S. Patent Office and other countries
Marca Registrada

Original Text:	Jack Messenger and Brigitte Lee
Photography:	Pete Bennett
Cover Photo:	© David Noton/International Stock
Editors:	Media Content Marketing, Inc.
Layout:	Media Content Marketing, Inc.
Cartography:	Ortelius Design

*Although we make every effort to ensure the accuracy of all infor-
mation in this book, changes do occur. If you find an error in this
guide, please let our editors know by writing to us at Berlitz Publishing Company, 400 Alexander Park, Princeton, NJ 08540-6306.
A postcard will do.*

ISBN 2-8315-7214-2
Revised 1998 – First Printing December 1998

Printed in Switzerland
019/812 REV

CONTENTS

- A (☛ in the text denotes a highly recommended sight

Bruges and Ghent

BRUGES, GHENT, AND THE BELGIANS

The land that is now Belgium has been coveted and fought over for thousands of years. The modern visitor can still catch the faint echo of all the armies that have battled and died on the soil of Flanders. Today, the nation that once was criss-crossed by foreign forces is traversed by millions of visitors, most of whom are on their way to holidays elsewhere in Europe. More and more travellers, however, have learned the secrets of Belgium, having discovered for themselves two of the country's greatest treasures—Bruges and Ghent.

What is it about these cities that sets them apart? There are many reasons, chief among them that the histories of Bruges and Ghent are everywhere written in their streets and buildings, their art, and their culture. Bruges, in particular, is justifiably famous for its sheer beauty; it is certainly one of the most uniformly picturesque cities one is ever likely to visit. Ghent contains areas of great historical as well as artistic interest, but also has the feel of a vibrant town with plenty of other things on its mind. Combine this with the compactness of the two cities' geography, which means that visitors can explore both cities on foot, by bike, and even by water with ease. It is, quite simply, a joy to wander through Bruges and Ghent, taking in the atmosphere of each place, knowing that the next highlight is just around the corner.

Water forms an important part of the landscape and economy of Ghent and Bruges. Canals link both cities to one another, as well as to the coast and important industrial centres. In the country as a whole, the extensive canal network carries more goods than do the railways. A leisurely

Handmade chocolates tempt the visitor from behind beautifully arranged shop windows.

cruise along the canals of the old cities is an experience not to be missed by the visitor and one of the best ways of viewing the wonderful cityscapes. The canal-side roads and paths make for excellent walking and cycling, so there is no need for a car.

Belgium is a compact country (less than 325 km/200 miles across at its widest point), so nothing seems very far from anywhere else. Most of the other places of interest listed in this guide are within a few miles of Bruges and Ghent, themselves connected by a half-hour train journey. Those places further away are easily accessible, thanks to the country's superb railways—in 1835 Belgium ran the first train in continental Europe.

It is, of course, the people that really constitute a city: there are about 115,000 in Bruges and just over 210,000 in Ghent. The majority of the population is Roman Catholic, and the virtues of community cohesion in work and play make up much of what it is to be Belgian. Tradition and family life are important, and people take their work and their pleasures seriously—which explains why the country produces over 750 of its own beers. Something else that figures prominently in Belgium is the museum. The Belgians, at least in their civic life, have a passion for collecting and recording; Bruges and Ghent share in this national idiosyncrasy, with some superb museums and galleries to enjoy. They also have a rich calendar of events (see page 88), including Bruges' spectacular Procession of the Holy Blood and the Ghent Flower Festival.

Eating and drinking in Belgium are mostly hearty events and form an important part of life. Belgian cuisine is justly famous throughout the world, both for its quality and its quantity (you'll never go hungry in Belgium), and there are lots of fine restaurants in Bruges and Ghent. An intrinsic part

An essential delight: a ride through cobblestone streets in a horse-drawn carriage.

of everyday eating, however, is the unique Belgian chip (*patates frites*), which is available everywhere. Equally ubiquitous are the exquisite Belgian chocolates you will see in beautifully mouth-watering shop displays.

The Belgians have evolved a strong sense of pride in their achievements and their history. Each town and city—Bruges and Ghent in particular—have had distinctive roles in the development of the area, and, before the foundation of the Belgian state in 1830, virtually constituted autonomous city-states. Nationhood itself is a fiercely debated issue in Belgium. Both Bruges and Ghent are in the north in Flemish-speaking Flanders, but a large part of the country is inhabited by the French-speaking Walloons (there is also a small area of mainly German-speaking inhabitants). This linguistic and cultural mix is most evident in the multi-lingualism of the cities' residents: nearly all speak English and French.

Bruges and Ghent also take their visitors seriously. Tourist offices are friendly and informative, and in cafés, bars, hotels, and restaurants you will be served courteously, with good humour and patience. Whether you are staying for a weekend or using the two cities as bases for a longer tour, Bruges and Ghent will reward you with beauty, fascinating history, and a warm welcome.

One of Bruges' courteous and hard-working waiters takes a well-earned rest.

A BRIEF HISTORY

The nation of Belgium only came into being in 1830, but both Bruges and Ghent can lay claim to a long, distinguished history. The prehistory of the region begins with the Belgae, a group of Celtic peoples who, along with other tribes, lived here from Neolithic times. In the first of numerous occupations throughout the centuries, the Belgae were conquered in 51 B.C. by the Romans under Julius Caesar. His account of the conquest of Gaul (as it was known) is recorded in his *Gallic Wars*. The small settlement that was to become Ghent dates from around this time.

The Kingdom of the Franks

The decay of the Roman empire early in the fifth century led to Roman withdrawal from Gaul, much of which succumbed to the ambitions of the Franks, who had been settling in the region for the past two centuries. They set up their Merovingian kingdom around Tournai in the south, while to the north and east the region was divided between Franks, Frisians, and Saxons.

The conversion to Christianity of the Frankish King Clovis in 498 led to a gradual northward spread of the new faith, until the whole region became Christian. The city of Ghent proved one of the last bastions of paganism in Gaul. The settlement started to develop in the seventh century when St. Amandus founded two abbeys here, but not before a few devout Ghent pagans had thrown the missionary into the River Scheldt. The first mention of Bruges also dates from the seventh century, though little else is known about its origins except that the name possibly comes from the Vikings.

Political unity succeeded religious unity when, in 768, the Frankish King Charlemagne established a unified kingdom. He went on to found by military and diplomatic means a Eu-

The trade guilds were powerful political forces: this banner represents the clothiers.

ropean empire, culminating in his coronation by the Pope in 800 as the first Holy Roman Emperor. On Charlemagne's death in 814, however, the empire was divided between his three grandsons. The division left a narrow strip of Europe, including the Low Countries (Belgium, Luxembourg, and the Netherlands), sandwiched between French- and German-speaking nations, determining the bloody destiny of Belgium beyond World War II.

The Golden Age of Bruges and Ghent

The area came under the nominal rule of a succession of German and French kings, but real power was in the hands of local nobles, who tried their best to weaken the hold over them by the French and German feudal kingdoms. Some of these lords were indeed more wealthy than their rulers and bequeathed charters of autonomous rights to towns in exchange for taxes and military help. Baldwin I (known menacingly as Iron Arm) built a castle at Bruges in the ninth century, and from there pursued a fierce expansionist policy to establish the principality of Flanders. The first castle of Gravensteen in Ghent dates from around the late tenth century. In the 11th century, the succession for Flanders passed to Robert the Frisian, who made Bruges his capital.

Despite the ongoing power struggles, the cloth towns of Flanders flourished in the 12th and 13th centuries. Ghent developed into the largest town in Western Europe, while Bruges drew a population as large as that of medieval London, trading with the Orient, the Middle East, and the rest of Europe. International banks made Bruges their headquarters, foreign embassies located there, and the first stock exchange in Europe was held in the city. Wool was vital to the economy: Bruges, Ghent, and Ieper (Ypres) all prospered from the export of their manufactured cloth, and depended for raw material on imported wool from England. Bruges monopolized the trade in wool, and, as a result, came to head the Hanseatic League, an extremely powerful economic alliance of towns trading with England. During what became known as the "Joyful Entry" into Bruges in 1301, Queen Joan of Navarre marvelled at the rich apparel of the citizens: "I thought I was the only queen, but there are hundreds more around me!" The prosperity of Bruges reached a peak early in the 14th century.

As the 13th and 14th centuries progressed, however, the tension between proto-capitalist cloth merchants with every reason for keeping in with the king of England (because he controlled the supply of wool), and their lords who usually sided with the French king, meant that the cloth towns of Flanders saw frequent hostilities. The most famous conflict became known as the "Bruges Matins." The French king, Philip the Fair, had invaded Flanders and appointed a governor whose taxation and suppression of the powerful guilds of Bruges were so severe that on the night of 17–18 May 1302 the city revolted, led by Pieter de Coninck and Jan Breydel. The resentful rebels killed everyone they thought to be French. In the same year the French were also defeated by the Flemish, at the Battle of the Golden Spurs near Courtrai (*Kortrijk*). Shortly afterwards, Ghent provided a focus for further rebellion. Ghent had been ruled since the late tenth century by a small council in line with the French king. This incensed the independently-minded guilds, and in 1337 a wool merchant named Jacob van Artevelde led the people of the city and other Flemish towns in revolt. He ruled Ghent as dictator until his murder in 1345.

In 1384 the region became part of the Burgundian kingdom. Philip the Good of Burgundy became the Count of Flanders in 1419 and ushered in a new kind of rule. He administered his possessions in Burgundy from Bruges, where artists such as van Eyck and Memling were patronized and the court became renowned for its splendour. In 1429 Philip received his fiancée, Isabella of Portugal, in Bruges—an occasion of sumptuous ostentation.

Ghent also came under Burgundian control, but objected to the constant attempts to suppress its guilds. In July 1453, many thousands of Ghent citizens were killed in the Battle of Gavère and city dignitaries had to beg for mercy. Charles the

Bold, Philip's successor, and his bride Margaret of York enjoyed a sumptuous wedding in Bruges, when, it was said, the fountains spouted Burgundian wine. But the splendour of Charles's reign did not last, and his death precipitated another French invasion of the south of the Burgundian kingdom. The people of Flanders took the

Artist Hans Memling watches over the square that bears his name.

opportunity to kidnap Charles's daughter Mary, and forced her to renew their civic rights (curtailed by Philip) in a charter before they would help fight the French.

The Habsburgs

Maximilian of Austria married Mary and assumed full control of the region on her death in 1482. The era of the Habsburgs had begun. The burghers of Bruges still had the nerve to incarcerate Maximilian himself briefly in 1488, exacting further promises to acknowledge their rights, but Maximilian reneged on these as soon as he was released. His grandson Charles V, born in Ghent in 1500, continued a policy of favouring Antwerp rather than the cloth towns of Flanders— despite Bruges' reception of him with great pomp and splendour in 1520. The policy exacerbated the economic decline of Bruges and Ghent; as well as their own mutual antagonism, they now faced stiff competition from the cloth manufactures in England.

Bruges' death blow came when the River Zwin silted up, cutting off the town from the sea and ending its international trade. Bruges did not awake from its economic slumber until the 19th century.

The Reformation

The movement we call the Reformation was bound to have had strong appeal for the merchants and people of Flanders. It stressed the rights of individuals to read and interpret the Word of God for themselves, thanks to the invention of the printing press, and questioned the clergy's power to promulgate a world view controlled by the State and Church in alliance. With the advent of Calvin and Luther, pressure for reform turned into outright revolt, leading to the establishment of alternative churches: Protestantism was born. The

Low Countries were particularly receptive to new ideas, as rich merchants chafed against the strictures of a rigidly hierarchical social system, while the artisanal guilds had always resented any royal authority. Charles V's abdication in 1555 meant that the Low Countries passed to his Catholic son, Philip II of Spain, and bloody conflict ensued.

Philip and his sister Margaret harshly repressed Protestantism and tried to reinstate the authority of the Catholic Church. The 1565 harvest failure caused widespread famine and led to the Iconoclastic Fury, when workers ran riot among the Catholic Churches, sacking and destroying everything. Frightened for their own positions, the nobility sided with Margaret and Philip; in 1567 Philip sent in the army to the Netherlands. The "Pacification of Ghent" was signed in the city in 1576: the treaty forced Philip II to concede 17 provinces. A subsequent war between the Spanish and the Dutch Protestants, led by William the Silent, resulted in the 1579 partitioning of the Netherlands—with the Protestant north gaining independence and the Catholic south siding with the Spanish. This partition corresponds more or less to today's border between Belgium and the Netherlands.

War of the Spanish Succession

The Habsburg dynasty in Spain ended in 1700 with the death without heirs of Charles II. Charles had specified that Philip V of Anjou should succeed him, but the Habsburg Leopold II of Austria had other ideas. He did not like the thought of the grandson of the king of France ruling Spain, thus uniting the two kingdoms under one dynasty. He was prepared to have his army die for this belief and the resulting war lasted from 1701 to 1714. The treaty that terminated the war signed over the Spanish Netherlands and Belgium to Austrian rule. They remained in Austrian hands under Marie Theresa of Austria, and Belgium prospered through an arrangement whereby its trade was subsidized by Austria. It was during this period that architecture, lacemaking, and art flourished, and Ghent's economic revival began with the establishment of the cotton industry. As so often the case, however, distribution of the new wealth was limited to the aristocracy and the hardworking merchants, while the majority of the population barely managed to scrape a living.

In 1780, Marie Theresa died and was succeeded by her son Joseph II. Although he fancied himself a radical ruler and did institute several enlightened, secularizing reforms, his lack of consultation and his "top-down" approach to change created widespread resentment. Sporadic rebellions occurred from 1788, and in 1790 the "United States of Belgium" was proclaimed, winning recognition from Britain and the Netherlands. The fledgling nation was defeated a year later by the forces of the new Austrian Emperor, Leopold II.

Lying in state: the exquisite mausoleums of Charles and Mary of Burgundy.

French Invasion and Independence

Despite receiving military assistance from a Belgian contingent against the Austrians in 1792, the army of revolutionary France invaded Belgium and the Netherlands two years later and occupied the annexed countries for the next 20 years, though not without some benefit to Belgium. The country was divided into *départements* along French lines and the old absolutist system of government was removed. Important and unjust aspects of Church, State, and taxation were reformed or abolished. There was also rapid subsidized industrialization, with France as the main market for Belgian manufactures.

But no country likes to be controlled by another. Rebellions occurred from 1798 onwards, and after the final defeat of Napoleon at Waterloo in 1815, the Congress of Vienna perpetuated Belgium's subjugation by giving control of the country to the Dutch House of Orange. It was not until the revolution in 1830 that a lastingly free Belgian state was created. In 1831, the London Conference recognized the independence of Belgium and established it as a constitutional monarchy. Leopold I was awarded the crown.

Armageddon — Twice

Throughout the 19th century, Belgium modernized, immersing itself in the Industrial Revolution. In 1907, the completion of a new canal again linked Bruges to the sea and attracted industry. The city was also slowly being rediscovered by British travellers on their way to see the site of Waterloo. Ghent revived, becoming a major economic centre. Yet tensions between the linguistic groupings within the new country became more obvious as persistent social difficulties failed to be resolved. Also, the living conditions for working people were often appalling, and there was dreadful famine in Flanders from 1845 to 1848.

Historical Landmarks

51 B.C.	Roman conquest of Gaul.
A.D. 498	Conversion to Christianity of Frankish King Clovis.
700s	Foundation of Ghent abbeys; first mention of Bruges.
768	Charlemagne's unified kingdom is established.
800s	Castle built at Bruges.
814	Death of Charlemagne and division of empire.
864	Baldwin becomes first Count of Flanders.
1302	Bruges Matins and Battle of the Golden Spurs.
1337	Revolt of Ghent against French rule.
1384	Flanders becomes part of Burgundian kingdom.
1419	Philip the Good of Burgundy made Count of Flanders.
1453	Battle of Gavère.
1482	Habsburg reign begins with Maximilian of Austria.
1555	Charles V abdicates; Philip II succeeds.
1701–14	War of the Spanish Succession.
1780	Marie Therese dies; Joseph II accedes.
1790	Proclamation of United States of Belgium.
1794	French invade and occupy country for 20 years.
1815	Napoleon defeated, Waterloo; Congress of Vienna.
1830	Belgian revolution and independence.
1914–18	World War I; Germans invade neutral Belgium.
1940	Nazi Germany launched blitzkrieg, Belgium.
1948	Benelux fully formed, with Belgium as member.
1949	Belgium joins NATO.
1957	Belgium becomes founding member of EEC.
1977	Establishment of three federal regions.
1989	Regional governments created.
1993	Albert II becomes king.
1994	New Belgian Constitution adopted, establishing Belgium as a federal state.

At the time when Bruges became the capital of Flanders almost half the population was dependent on charity. In need of a scapegoat, the predominantly Flemish-speaking (and increasingly prosperous) north agitated increasingly for independence from the (French-speaking) Walloon south.

Instead of attending to the problems of his country, the new king of Belgium, Leopold II (1865 to 1909) devoted most of his time to personal interests, including a private slave colony in the Belgian Congo. Albert I, nephew to Leopold II, succeeded him in 1909. During his reign, World War I gripped Belgium for four years. In 1914, the German army invaded despite Belgium's neutrality, forcing the king to remove to a narrow remaining strip of unoccupied Belgium. His resistance to the invaders gained him international friends. The northern front of the war extended roughly diagonally across the country, with the most infamous—and bloodiest—of battles taking place around Ieper (Ypres) in southern Flanders. The German defeat won Belgium considerable reparations and some new territory.

It might have been expected that the experience of war would have drawn the Belgian nation together, especially when King Albert proclaimed a series of reforms meant to improve equality between the Flemish and the Walloons. But as Fascism was already working its way through both communi-

Tyne Cot military cemetery in Flanders, where the armies of the dead dwell.

ties, they grew more antagonistic. In 1940, the Nazi German army launched their blitzkrieg through Belgium, occupying it in a mere three weeks (Bruges and Ghent suffered little damage, though the former's new canal had to be repaired extensively). A resistance movement formed from around 1941, including an underground network to protect Belgium's Jews. However, the behaviour of the king, Leopold III, eager to accommodate the invaders, caused much controversy after the war as Belgium sought to repair itself. In 1950, the people voted by a narrow margin to ask the king home from exile, but Leopold decided to abdicate in favour of his son, Baudouin I.

Regionalization

After forming Benelux, an economic union with the Netherlands and Luxembourg, Belgium went on to join the European Community in 1957, with Brussels the capital of the organization. The country at last divested itself of the Belgian Congo (now Zaire) in 1960. Internal political events since the end of World War II have been dominated by the continuing friction between the Flemish and Walloons. In 1977, three federal regions were established—Wallonia, Flanders, and Brussels—in the hope that greater self-determination would ease the tensions between the groups, and in 1989 the regional governments were created, each with responsibility for everything except matters concerning social security, defence, and foreign policy. A new Belgian constitution was adopted in 1994, establishing Belgium as a federal state.

In practice, the universal courtesy of Belgians means that visitors today will see little sign of community conflict. Bruges' ambitious restoration of the medieval city now attracts tourists from all over the world. Similarly, Ghent is undertaking an intensive restoration programme in a move to attract more visitors and ensure its continued prosperity.

WHERE TO GO

Bruges and Ghent are roughly 50 km (30 miles) apart; you should have no difficulty in exploring either of them on foot. Bruges is made for walking: it is very compact, with attractions clearly signposted. It has also been dubbed the "Venice of the North," and while this comparison is unfair to both places, it should be no surprise that canal cruises are one of the best ways of viewing the city: central Bruges has 10 km (6 miles) of canals, with 4 km (2½ miles) accessible by boat tour. Ghent is a bit larger than Bruges, but most of its historic attractions are clustered together within walking distance from one another. It too offers canal cruises in the summer.

BRUGES

Bruges, the capital of West Flanders, is probably the most popular tourist destination in Belgium, so be prepared for

A tour through the large canal system in Bruges is a great way to see the city.

large crowds in the summer. In describing the city's attractions certain words unavoidably spring to mind, namely, "charming," "picturesque," and "delightful." Bruges is all of these, which is why ambling through the city is such a pleasure. It is not built on a grand scale calculated to awe the visitor, but views assail you from every side, and around each corner it seems there is something else to delight the eye and fire the imagination. Paradoxically, it was

Bruges' many flags proudly fly in front of the city's typical red-shutter houses.

Bruges' five-century economic decline that preserved the buildings we now enjoy, as there was never any money to demolish and rebuild. The badly dilapidated city was "discovered" by visitors in the 19th century, and in the quieter residential quarters you can still sense what it must have been like to walk through the forgotten streets of a forgotten town — your footsteps ringing on the cobblestones while church bells chime and a horse's hooves echo from a neighbouring street.

One of the first things to strike visitors today is the harmonious appearance of the architecture. The characteristic step gables of the houses may often be a bit worn through age, but this only adds to their charm. You'll notice that most buildings are constructed in brick, with their shutters and woodwork painted in traditional Bruges red. Bruges is now so beautifully restored that you may briefly find yourself yearning for something less perfect just by way of contrast; Belgians themselves describe the place as an outdoor museum. Still, you are certain to enjoy the walk described below; you should also take pleasure in improvising some of your own (perhaps simply following the canals, or tracing the path of the city walls with their big, imposing gates). Horse-drawn carriages can also be hired in the Burg.

Bruges' Old Town is almost an island encircled by canals. At the centre of the island and at the heart of the city's life is the **Markt,** Bruges' main square. It is from here that our walk begins. None of the sights described in this book is more than 2 km (1 mile) or so from where you now stand. But before you set off, take time to look around the Markt. It may be the end of the 20th century (as the cars prove), but not much has changed since some of the civic buildings and houses that you can see were constructed; it's not hard to imagine what the place would have looked like in the city's bustling golden age.

South from the Markt

On the southeast side of the square, dominating the city, is the magnificent complex of brick buildings known as the **Belfort-Hallen** (Bell Tower and Covered Market). One of the first priorities of any visitor is to ignore the 1-metre (3-foot) lean of the 90-metre (300-foot) belfry and climb its 366 steps for a breathtaking view of the town and surrounding countryside (the best time is early morning or late afternoon). The belfry dates from the 13th century, when Bruges was at the height of its prosperity, but the final storey (with the clock) is 15th-century. Inside is a second-floor treasury where the town seal and charters were safely kept behind the intricate Romanesque grilles built in 1292, each requiring nine separate keys to open them. You may already have heard the 47-bell carillon (which weighs 27 tons and hangs above you in the tower). The belfry is a superb landmark when you're finding your way around. The covered market and courtyard, also dating from the 13th century, would have been crammed with traders, the air heavy with the scent of spices brought by the Venetian merchants. There was originally a canal below the market, so goods could be loaded and unloaded. City statutes were announced from the balcony over the entrance.

At the centre of the Markt a few yards away is a 19th-century monument to the heroes of the Bruges Matins (see page 13); Pieter de Coninck and Jan Breydel are stained green with age, but they still look suitably determined.

The 13th-century cloth halls were once located on the east side of the Markt, now the site of the Neo-Gothic **Provinciaal Hof** (housing the West Flanders provincial government, which is not open to visitors). The **Craenenburg,** on the opposite side of the square, was where Emperor Maximilian of Austria was briefly imprisoned by the city in 1488: the understandably disgruntled emperor did his best ever afterward to promote trade through Antwerp at the expense of Bruges' economy (see page 15). On the same side of the square, at the corner of Sint-

The cobblestone Markt is bounded by centuries-old houses with step gables.

Amandsstraat, is the beautiful 15th-century brick building, the **Huis Bouchoute.**

☛ *The Burg*

A stroll down Breidelstraat, located in the southeast corner of the Markt (next to the Halle), will take you past De Garre, the shortest road in Bruges; if you're in need of refreshment, there's a cosy 100-beer bar at the end called the Staminee de Garre. Breidelstraat leads to the **Burg,** one of the finest medieval squares in Europe, named after the castle built by Baldwin Iron Arm. Which building in the square is the most splendid? It's a hard choice. On the corner of Breidelstraat and the Burg is the ornate Baroque **Proosdij** (Deanery), formerly the palace of the bishops of Bruges, dating from 1666. Its parapet is lined with urns and topped with a handsome female personification of justice armed with sword and scales. The building stands on the site of St. Donaaskerk (St. Donatien's), a Carolingian-style church built around 900. A miniature stone replica of the church stands under the trees of the Burg, to the right of the building as you face it. The **Stadhuis** (Town Hall) situated on the south side of the Burg was constructed between 1376 and 1420. It is one of the oldest town halls in Belgium and a Gothic masterpiece, its delicately traced windows framed within pilasters topped with octagonal turrets. If you stand close to the building, its statues and spiral chimneys seem to be curving down over you, the detailing of the sandstone façade becoming even more impressive. The statues on the façade (modern copies of those painted by van Eyck and destroyed by the French in the 1790s) are of the counts of Flanders.

The exterior of the Stadhuis promises great things, and the interior of the magnificent town hall will certainly not let you down. Bluestone stairs lead from the flag-draped entrance hall to the first-floor Gothic Hall, a splendid room that witnessed the first meeting of the States General, set up in 1464 by the dukes of Burgundy to regulate provincial contributions to the treasury. The vaulted oak ceiling (begun in 1385 and finished in 1402), with its preposterously long pendant keystones at the junctions of the arches, is richly decorated in tones of brown, black, maroon, and gold, surrounding painted scenes from the New Testament. The murals, depicting important events in the city's history, were painted by the De Vriendt brothers in 1905 after the original 1410 wall decorations were lost. The small, delicate balcony near the entrance door was for the town pipers and other musicians. The hall is used for civil ceremonies, receptions, and weddings. An adjoining room displays old coins, documents, and other artefacts relating to the history of Bruges.

To the right of the Stadhuis as you face it is the small gilded entrance to the **Basiliek van het Heilig Bloed** (Basilica of the Holy Blood), the three-arched façade of which was completed by 1534, making it a mere youth in comparison with the Stadhuis. Its ornate stone carvings and gilded statues of angels, knights, and their ladies stand below two closely adjoining and strangely Islamic-looking towers of great delicacy. The interior of the basilica is divided into two chapels, a 12th-century Romanesque lower chapel and

People can still be married in the beautiful Gothic Hall of the Stadhuis.

a younger Gothic upper chapel, providing a dramatic contrast in styles. The lower chapel is a study in shadows, with austere, unadorned lines, typically uncompromising Romanesque pillars, and little decoration except for a relief carving over an interior doorway depicting the baptism of St. Basil (an early Church Father). St. Basil's relics were brought back from Palestine by Robert II, the Count of Flanders. The worn, faded carving is child-like in style, its naivety emphasized by the two mismatched columns supporting it.

Access to the upper chapel is through a beautiful late-Gothic doorway. Ascending by an elegant, broad 16th-century spiral staircase, you can enter the upper chapel beneath the organ case. The lines of the chapel may have been spoiled somewhat by over-eager 19th-century decoration and murals, but the greater impression is of warmth and richness. The ceiling looks like an upturned boat and the room is flooded with a golden light. The bronze-coloured pulpit is a curious sight, bearing a remarkable resemblance to a cored and stuffed tomato. In a small side chapel you'll find the holy relic from which the

church derives its name. Flemish knight Dietrich of Alsace returned from the Second Crusade in the Holy Land in 1149 and brought with him a crystal phial believed to contain some drops of Christ's blood. Soon venerated all over medieval Eu-

The entryway to the upper chapel in the Basilica of the Holy Blood.

The Procession of the Holy Blood is an Ascension Day event recalling centuries of veneration.

rope, it is still brought out each Friday for the faithful. The dried blood turned to liquid at regular intervals for many years —declared to be a miracle by Pope Clement V. The phial is stored in a richly and rather heavily ornate silver tabernacle presented by the archdukes of Spain in 1611. The fame of the relic and the veneration in which it was held can be partially recaptured every May on Ascension Day, when it is processed through the city in the famous *Heilig-Bloedprocessie* (Procession of the Holy Blood), the preeminent festival of West Flanders. A small treasury off the chapel displays the flamboyant gold-and-silver reliquary used to transport the phial during the procession, together with a 16th-century triptych by Pieter Pourbus depicting the Brotherhood of the Holy Blood.

Opposite the Basilica, the Bruges Tourist Office (indicated by a large white-and-green sign) occupies the **Paleis Van het Brugse Vrije** (the Freeman of Bruges' Mansion), an early 18th-century Neo-Classical building on the site of an older structure that formerly housed the law courts. (At the rear of the building overlooking the canal are the remains of an earlier, attractive 16th-century façade.)

Adjoining this building is the statue-laden, Renaissance-style **Oude Civiele Griffie** (Old Recorder's House), completed in 1537. Note how the sinuously curved and scrolled gables contrast with the older, linear step gables of most of architecture found in Bruges. The **Brugse Vrije Museum** located inside the Old Recorder's House has one main exhibit—the great black-marble-and-oak Renaissance "Emperor Charles" chimneypiece, designed by the painter Lanceloot Blondeel in tribute to Charles V, started in 1528 and finished in 1531. This is one of the most memorable artworks in Bruges; it should not be missed. The carving is on a monumental scale, covering an entire wall and joining the ceiling with carved tendrils and caskets. A statue of Charles in full armour, wearing the emblem of the Order of the Golden Fleece, is in the centre. Forty-six coats of arms and ribbons of wood also appear on it. Among many of the scenes, the design depicts the defeat of the French at Pavia and the biblical story of Susanna and the Elders. The intricate craftsmanship of the piece is superb and quite overwhelming, but the handholds for gentlemen to use while drying their boots are the sort of domestic touch everyone remembers.

Around Vismarkt

If you wander through the Renaissance arch joining the Oude Civiele Griffie and the Stadhuis, you can follow the Blinde Ezelstraat (Blind Donkey Street) across the bridge until you reach the colonnaded **Vismarkt** (Fishmarket). Built in 1821, this structure covers a still-thriving market that sells fresh fish from the North Sea. Along both sides of the canal are pretty streets with lovely views. On Groene Rei (left at the bridge) you will find the 1634 **Pelicaanhuis** (Pelican House). Easily identified by its Pelican emblem over the door, this was once a hospital or almshouse. Such almshouses can be found all over Bruges: they were built by the guilds of the city to shelter the sick, elderly, and poor. They are usually low, whitewashed cottages like the ones in Zwarte-Leertouwerstraat (take the last right turn in Groene Rei).

Back behind the Vismarkt, you can wander through Huidenvettersplein (Tanners' Square), which has become something of a growth area for cafés and excellent restaurants. **Huidenvettershuis** (Tanners' Guild Hall), the turreted house, was built in 1630. Beyond the square, **Rozenhoedkaai** (Rosary Quay) is one of the places where boat cruises depart; do stop to enjoy the view from the quay. The River Dijver—a branch of the Rei—begins at **St. J Nepomucenusbrug** (the Bridge of St. John of Nepomuk). A statue portrays the good man himself, the highly appropriate patron saint of bridges. Along the bank, the tree-lined Dijver—site of a weekend flea market—passes superb old houses and crosses the canal into Gruuthusestraat. On the left is a complex of museums: the Groeninge, the Brangwyn, and the Gruuthuse.

Groeninge Museum

The **Groeninge Museum** (Museum of Fine Art) contains some of the great works of the Flemish Primitives, including van Eyck's portrait of his supercilious-looking wife Margareta, so

The Groeninge Museum garden provides a typically Flemish scene.

Bruges Museums

Brangwyn Museum: *Dijver 16*. The art of Frank Brangwyn, plus small lace museum. Open Apr–Sep 9:30am–5pm; Oct–Mar 9:30am–12:30pm, 2–5pm. BF80. (See page 33)

Bruges Vrije Museum: *Burg 11*. Magnificent Renaissance chimneypiece. Open Apr–Sep Tue–Sun 9:30am–12:30pm, 1:15–5pm; Oct–Mar 9:30am–12:30pm, 2–5pm; closed January. BF100. (See page 30)

Groeninge Museum: *Dijver 12*. Superb medieval Flemish paintings. Open Apr–Sep 9:30am–5pm; Oct–Mar Wed–Mon 9:30am–12:30pm, 2–5pm BF200. (See page 31)

Gruuthuse Museum: *Dijver 17*. Beautiful period house. Apr–Sep 9:30am–5pm; Oct–Mar Wed–Mon 9:30am–12:30pm, 2–5pm. BF130. (See page 34)

Guido Gezelle Museum: *Rolweg 64*. House and garden of Flemish poet. Open Apr–Sep 9:30am–12:30pm, 1:15–5pm; Oct–Mar Wed–Mon 9:30am–12:30pm, 2–5pm. BF40.

Kantcentrum (Lace Centre): *Peperstraat 3*. Lace museum and demonstrations of lacemaking. Open Mon–Fri 10am–noon, 2–6pm; Sat 10am–noon, 2–5pm. Closed Sundays and holidays. Demonstrations every afternoon. BF60.

Memling Museum: *Mariastraat 38*. The paintings of the Flemish master. Open Apr–Sep 9:30am–5pm; Oct–Mar Thurs–Tues 9:30am–12:30pm, 2–5pm BF100. (See page 37)

Museum Potterie: *Potterierei 79*. Baroque chapel, ecclesiastical art and furnishings. Apr–Sep 9:30am–5pm, 1:15–5pm; Oct–Mar Wed–Mon 9:30am–12:30pm, 2–5pm. BF60.

Stedelijk Museum voor Volkskunde (Folklore): *Rolweg 40*. Period-style almshouses. Apr–Sep 9:30am–5pm; Oct–Mar Wed–Mon 9:30am–12:30pm, 2–5pm. BF80. (See page 46)

Straffe Hendrik Brewery: *Walplein 26*. Small brewery and museum. Open for guided tours Apr–Sep 10am–5pm continuously; Oct–Mar 11am & 3pm BF140 (inc. drink). (See page 40)

Combination ticket for Groeninge, Gruuthuse, Brangwyn, and Memling museums BF400. Family tickets available for all museums.

typical of the painter's incredible realism, and Bosch's deeply disturbing *Last Judgement,* with the fires of hell ablaze. *The Judgement of Cambyses,* painted by Gerard David in 1498, depicts the judicial skinning of a corrupt judge while detached onlookers coolly observe the entire proceedings. Some other treasures include Memling's glorious *Moreel Tryptych* depicting St. Christopher, with portraits in the side panels, and his *St. John Altarpiece.* In addition, there are magnificent portraits by van der Goes, Rogier van der Weyden, and also Petrus Christus, as well as paintings by unknown masters, many of them depicting views of the city. However, the greatest work in the museum is undoubtedly van Eyck's *Madonna with Canon George Van der Paele,* where the textures and folds of clothes and carpets are reproduced with breathtaking effect. There is also work from later periods, including a landscape by James Ensor, enigmatic work by Magritte, and some recently acquired Flemish Expressionists—but it's the early Flemish artists that steal the show. The 15 or so rooms of the museum are well laid out, with multilingual labels.

Brangwyn Museum

At number 16, the **Brangwyn Museum** is named after its extensive collection of the art of Sir Frank Brangwyn, a Welsh artist who was born in Bruges in 1867 and who bequeathed his work to the city when he died in 1956. He

Over a barrel: The Straffe Hendrik Brewery provides a free drink with your visit.

The Gruuthuse Museum boasts many rooms decorated in the styles of different eras.

was a disciple of the Arts and Crafts movement, and its influence is apparent in the etchings, prints, and rugs on display. Brangwyn was an apprentice to the movement's greatest figure, William Morris, before becoming a war artist in World War I. The museum has a collection of paintings by Brangwyn and also some of his furniture. A small **Lace Museum** in the same building comprises a series of chandeliered apartments, each exhibiting incredibly detailed examples of the art of lace-making, particularly from the 19th century.

Gruuthuse Museum

In the courtyard at the rear of the Brangwyn Museum you can see Rik Poot's sculptures of the *Four Horsemen of the Apocalypse,* a scary combination of robotic armour and animal skeletons. The oldest bridge in Bruges (with a pronounced arch and cobblestones) connects the courtyard to the **Gruuthuse Museum,** so called because the original owners had rights to tax the "gruut" used in brewing beer ("gruut" refers to the herbs, plants, and barley used in the brewing of beer). The building itself is one of the museum's best exhibits—a splendid mansion of red brick. Built in the 15th century, it has twice sheltered fugitive English kings: both King Henry IV and Charles II stayed here, in 1471 and 1656, respectively. Inside the house, beautifully furnished in a variety of period styles, there is an evocative smell of polished wood. It boasts an exceptional collection of lacework, tapestries, and musical instruments, including a delicate spinet. Items are labelled in Flemish only, but you do not need labels to help you admire the imposing medieval kitchen or the magnificent fireplace and beamed ceiling in room 1. Room 5, with painted angels sculpted in the ceiling beams, provides some interesting views over the rooftops and into the courtyard of the mansion. There are also fine antique crossbows and a guillotine on display. Finally, the oratory (private chapel) in the mansion leads to the chancel of the adjoining Church of Our Lady, looking down into the church.

Onze Lieve Vrouwkerk

The 122-metre (400-foot) brick tower of **Onze Lieve Vrouwkerk** (Church of Our Lady), the highest in Belgium, once served as a kind of inland lighthouse for ships on their way to Bruges. The exterior of the church is a hodge-podge of different styles and slightly forbidding. More interesting is the interior, which is almost a warehouse of religious artworks and treasures—chief among which is the *Madonna and Child* by Michelangelo, originally intended for the cathedral in Siena and the only one of the sculptor's works to travel outside Italy during his lifetime. It was brought to Bruges by a Flemish merchant named Jan Moscroen. He must have earned thanks from numerous artists who found inspiration from the sculpture, including Albrecht Durer, who visited the church in 1521. The viewer today has to ignore the engulfing 18th-century altar supporting the sculpture, and the protective glass screen. You will notice that the Madonna is a subdued, preoccupied figure, while the infant leans nonchalantly on her knee.

There are some fine paintings here by Pieter Pourbus (*Last Supper* and *Adoration of the Shepherds*) and Gerard David (*Transfiguration*), but it is the chancel area that holds most interest, second to the Michelangelo. Here you can see the tombs of Charles the Bold and his daughter Mary of Burgundy, two fine examples of Renaissance carving. Both sarcophagi are richly decorated with coats of arms linked with floral motifs in copper-gilt gold, reds, and blues; the figures themselves (with domestic details like the pet dogs at Mary's feet) are also in copper gilt. Whether or not Charles and Mary are actually buried here is a matter of some dispute. Charles died in battle in Nancy in 1477 and it was difficult to identify the body. Mary (who died in a riding accident at the age of 25, bringing to a close the long reign of the dukes of Burgundy) may in fact be buried among a group of polychromed tombs in the choir which, quite astonishingly, were only discovered in 1979. You can see the frescoed tombs beneath your feet through windows in the floor and by means of mirrors in front of the sarcophagi.

Elsewhere in the church, you'll find the funerary chapel of Pieter Lanchals (see page 42), containing frescoed tombs in maroon and black as well as van Dyck's starkly atmospheric painting of *Christ on the Cross*. The splendid wooden gallery connecting the church to the

Michelangelo's "Madonna and Child" travelled to the Onze Lieve Vrouwkerk.

*There are many other artworks and precious relics to see
at the Onze Lieve Vrouwkerk as well.*

adjacent Gruuthuse Museum (see page 34) dates back to
the 15th century.

Sint-Janshospitaal

Opposite the church and through an archway you will find
Sint-Janshospitaal (St. John's Hospital). Constructed in
the 12th century, this is the oldest building in Bruges, and,
in what were once the wards of the hospital, there is an exhibition of historical documents and rather alarming surgi-
cal instruments. The 17th-century pharmacy has a carved
relief showing patients sleeping two to a bed. Amazingly,
the hospital only ceased functioning in the 19th century,
and there is a strong sense of tradition in the place, en-
hanced by the informative visitor centre (which also has an
attractive brasserie).

The old hospital church houses the **Memlingmuseum,**
largely devoted to six masterpieces by the Flemish master

The center panel of Memling's triptych "Mystic Marriage of St. Catherine."

Hans Memling. The museum is very small but is a must for any visitor to Bruges. Each of the exhibited works displays Memling's captivating attention to detail and mastery of realism. It's impossible to pick a favourite, but probably the most famous is the detailed *Reliquary of St. Ursula,* one of the greatest art treasures in the country. Commissioned by two sisters who worked in the church, the reliquary is in the form of a miniature Gothic chapel with Memling's painted panels in the positions of the windows. The *Mystic Marriage of St. Catherine* includes St. John the Evangelist and St. John the Baptist, both patron saints of the hospital, and it has been suggested that Saints Catherine and Barbara are portraits of Mary of Burgundy and Margaret of York. A painting by Jan Beerbloch depicts the more relaxed standards of hospital hygiene of the time: nurses sweep the floor and dogs wander the dormitories.

Around Mariastraat

If you head south along Mariastraat and look left along Nieuwe Gentweg, you will see some characteristically white almshouses, which have gardens open to the public. Also off Mariastraat is Stoofstraat, the narrowest street in Bruges—see if you can find it! The next turning on the right is Walstraat, a peaceful street of delightful 16th- and 17th-century gabled houses where lacemaking is still practised (outside

Painting the Flemish Way

Medieval Flanders bequeathed some of the most profound and best-loved works of painting to the world, the greatest of which can be seen in Bruges and Ghent. The brilliance of painters such as Bosch, Memling, and van Eyck sprang from the Gothic tradition that nurtured them. Gothic art was essentially a religious art of devotional paintings depicting the life of Christ, the Virgin Mary, and the saints, but it also came to place great emphasis on the accurate representation of the world, which was seen as God's creation and a vehicle for the sacred. (It is in this context that the full horror of the works of Bosch, where elements of the real world are combined and exaggerated until they become a thing of which nightmares are made, may be realized.)

Van Eyck retained the religious subject matter of the Gothic tradition, but brought the revolutionary medium of oil, enabling him to paint with greater control. No one before him had observed nature so minutely, or was capable of rendering observations so precisely. His portraits (often quite literally "warts and all") , along with those of Memling, and the paintings of artists such as Petrus Christus, Hugo van der Goes, and Pieter Pourbus, reinforce this truthfulness to appearance.

The combination of sacred theme and faithful depiction of the world was taken a stage farther a hundred years after van Eyck (famous for his painting *Madonna and the Donor Canon van de Paele,* and the portrait of his wife Magareta), in the work of Brueghel the Elder, whose paintings of biblical events are set in the recognizable peasant world of his time.

Nevertheless, the genius of an artist usually needs fertile soil in which to grow. For a long time the wealth of the Burgundian court and the merchant class of Bruges and Ghent was enough to pay for the commissioning of new works. Eventually, however, the economic centre of gravity moved northward to Antwerp (home to Rubens, who had van Dyck as his pupil) and the Netherlands, where the first sophisticated market for genre paintings developed. Inevitably, the influence of Flemish painting moved with the money. Yet its preoccupations were to filter through the artistic world for centuries to come.

on warm days). If your thirst for culture is overtaken by a thirst for something else, a short stroll will bring you to **Straffe Hendrik Brewery** at Walplein 26. Belgium is well known for its many hundreds of beers, and Bruges beers are exceptionally good. Straffe Hendrik, Flemish for "Strong Henry," has been brewing in the city since 1546 and in this location since 1856. It produces a light, highly fermented local beer of the same name. A 45-minute guided tour of the brewery museum will reveal how it's all done, and also includes an ascent to the roof, affording a good view over the gables of central Bruges. The building is suffused with a sweet smell from the brewing process. At the end of the visit, each person receives one drink in the congenial bar, lined with every conceivable shape of beer bottle.

☞ *Begijnhof*

South of the church along Mariastraat, follow the signposts to the **Begijnhof.** The country is famous for the number of its residences for tertiary religious orders, which were for unmarried or abandoned women (known as Beguines) who wished to live under a rule without having to commit themselves to the full vows of a nun. The women cared for the sick and made a living by lacemaking. The **Prinselijk Begijnhof ten Wijngaarde** ("Princely Beguinage of the Vineyard") was originally founded in 1245 by Margaret of Constantinople and remained a Beguine residence until very recently—it is now a Benedictine convent. The nuns wear the traditional clothes of the Beguines and prepare participants' costumes for the annual Procession of the Holy Blood. The convent is one of the most attractive of residences. Reached by a bridge over the canal and through an arch, it comprises a circle of white, 17th-century houses set around a courtyard of grass and trees that comes alive with daffodils each spring. In a city of charm replete with picturesque views, this is one of the most photographed places in Bruges. You can enter one of the former houses, which is now a small museum, and the church, built originally in 1245. Around the Begijnhof the layout of streets is as it was in the 17th century, so take time to wander around and enjoy the views.

Minnewater

The picturesque and understandably popular park and lake of **Minnewater** (Lake of Love) lie to the south of Walplein and Wijngaardplein. The lake was originally the outer harbour of Bruges, before the river silted up and cut off the city from the sea; you can still see the 15th-century *sashuis* (lock house). Just beyond the *sashuis,* the tower on the right is a remnant of old fortifications. The presence of swans on

Wander along 17th-century streets: when you're tired, retire to a cosy, vibrant 20th-century café.

the lake (so the story goes) stems from the time in 1448 when Emperor Maximilian was imprisoned in Bruges and his councillor Pieter Lanchals was beheaded. A swan featured in Lanchals' coat of arms, and the emperor ordered that the swans be kept on the canals of Bruges for evermore, serving as a reminder of the city's dreadful crime.

Another place to take a break: a bar with a selection of 300 different beers.

Steenstraat

If you feel doubtful about following your nose and the Belfry, you can return to the Markt via Mariastraat, Simon Stevinplein, and Steenstraat. Steenstraat is one of Bruges' gems, a beautiful street lined with entrancing gabled guildhouses. The Boat House and Mason's House on this street are topped with a gilded boat and bear, and masonic instruments, respectively. If you turn left on Steenstraat, you will come to **Sint-Salvatorskathedraal.** Parts of the building date from the 12th and 13th centuries, though the church was originally founded in the tenth century. The oldest parish church in Bruges, it has been a cathedral since 1834, replacing the city-centre cathedral destroyed by the French in the late 18th century. The enormous west tower, 99 metres (325 feet) tall, is a combination of period styles in a feat of cooperation down the centuries, starting with 12th-century Romanesque and ending with a steeple added in 1871. The Gothic interior of the church is curiously unfocused in de-

A safe harbour—the lake of Minnewater is lined with the remains of centuries-old fortifications.

sign and quite spartan, but the choir stalls and the Baroque rood screen showing God the Father are worth a look. The cathedral also has its own small museum, located off the right transept. Specializing in liturgical objects, it is worth visiting for its Flemish paintings, including work by Dirk Bouts and Pieter Pourbus.

Steenstraat will lead you back to the Markt. If you make a short detour south of Simon Stevinplein to Oude Burg, you will find the **Hof Van Watervliet.** The 16th-century buildings comprising the house have been much restored, but are still of particular interest, with former residents including the humanist scholar Erasmus and the exiled Charles II of England.

North from the Markt

The city north of the Markt, a much quieter area than the south, used to be home to the merchants of medieval Bruges. It was also where they conducted their business, for it was common practice to live and work in the same building. The avenues of elegant houses from this period are punctuated with grandiose mansions dating from the 18th century, and the canals here meet and diverge in broad highways of water: no wonder many visitors regard this part as their favourite section of the city.

☛ *Jan van Eyckplein*

A few minutes' walk north from the Markt along Vlamingstraat will lead you to Jan Van Eyckplein and the adjoining **Spiegelrei.** Bruges has many former harbours, and this one was the busiest of them all. The canal that terminates here once led to the Markt. It was also the commercial and diplomatic centre for medieval Bruges, and foreign consulates opened along the length of the Spiegelrei. There is a statue of the eponymous painter in the square, but the buildings are what really stand out. Jan looks directly at the most striking of these, namely the **Poorters Loge** (Burghers' Lodge). The pencil tower may be pointing heavenwards, but the building was in fact the meeting place and club of the wealthier merchants of Bruges. It dates from the 14th century; on its façade there is a statue of the jolly-looking bear that features in the city's coat of arms. It was also the emblem of a jousting club that held its events in the marketplace outside. To the right of the Poorters Loge as you face it is the 15th-century **Oud Tolhuis** (Customs House), where the tolls were levied by the dukes of Luxembourg and whose coats of arms are displayed on the façade. This delightful Gothic building now contains the city's library of 100,000 volumes and 600 manuscripts.

East of Jan van Eyckplein

From Jan van Eyckplein you can wander through the lovely street of Spinolarei right into Koningstraat and Sint-Maartensplein, where you will find **Sint-Walburgakerk** (Church of St. Walburga). This is a vigorously impressive Baroque church, built in 1643 by the Bruges Jesuit Pieter Huyssens, with a statue of St. Francis Xavier standing above the entrance door. The Baroque interior is for the most part quite unremarkable, except for the fabulous pulpit made by Artus Quellin the Younger. This graceful construction has twin stairways leading to a pulpit with a scalloped

The sculpted guardians of Bruges' honour are perpetually on the job.

canopy uplifted by trumpeting angels. It is a captivating piece of work that seems to lean unsupported far into the nave, like a tree bending over a river.

By crossing the canal and following Sint-Annarei south into Sint-Annakerkstraat, you will see the slender spire of **Sint-Annakerk** itself (Church of St. Anne), a 1624 Baroque replacement for the Gothic church demolished in 1561. Inside, the Baroque carving of the rood screen, confessionals, and pulpit, as well as the rich panelling, are all well worth viewing if you have time (and if the church is open). The unusual tower with the vaguely Oriental look visible from Sint-Annakerk belongs to the **Jeruzalemkerk,** located not in nearby Jeruzalemstraat as you may have expected, but in Peperstraat. The church is named after and modelled on the Church of the Holy Sepulchre in Jerusalem. Dating from 1428, it was erected by the Adornes family, originally merchants from Genoa, who had travelled on a pilgrimage to Jerusalem and were so impressed by the church that they built this one in Bruges. There is even a copy of Christ's memorial tomb in the crypt. It is a sombre, stark, and constricted church with very good examples of 15th- and 16th-century stained glass, some of which depict members of the Adornes family. In the nave you can see effigies of Anselmus Adornes and his wife. The altar is carved in a rather macabre fashion, with skulls and bones, and the cave-like atmosphere of the church is emphasized by the space behind the altar and above the crypt, which rises almost to the full height of the tower to create a rather eerie, artificial looking cavern.

Next door to the Jeruzalemkerk is the **Kantcentrum** (Lace Centre), a museum and workshop situated in the 15th-century Jeruzalemgodshuizen (almshouses) founded by the Adornes family. Here, fine examples of the craft of lacemaking and demonstrations by the workers and their pupils can be seen each day.

A sign points down Balstraat directing you towards the **Stedelijk Museum voor Volkskunde** (Folklore Museum).

The painstaking art of the bobbin lacemaker is not for the lazy, nor those in a hurry.

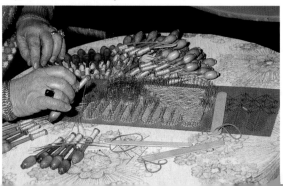

The museum, at Rolweg 40, can be found at the sign of De Zwarte Kat (Black Cat). It is located in delightful 17th-century almshouses built by the cobbler's guild, and the life of everyday West Flanders is recreated in the traditionally furnished interiors with art and objects of every kind, including a traditional ale house offering some respite for the weary walker.

West of Jan van Eyckplein

If you return to Jan van Eyckplein, you can then follow Acadamiestraat from the west side of the square. It joins Grauwerkerstraat, where you will find the elegant **Huis ter Beurze.** Now a bank, the 15th-century house belonged to the van der Beurze family. They rented rooms to many merchants of the city, who lived and worked in the house, and the family's name (rendered as "bourse" or "beurs") has since come to designate the place for a commercial stock exchange in many languages. The Genoese merchants in Bruges did their business in the building opposite, the **Natiehuis van Genua** (the Nation House of Genoa), built in 1441.

There are no grand churches in the order of the Onze Lieve Vrouwkerk or the Sint-Salvatorskathedraal north of the Markt, but **Sint-Jakobskerk** (Church of St. Jacob) in Sint-Jakobsstraat probably makes the most determined bid for grandiosity. Thanks to the generous gifts from the dukes of Burgundy, the 13th-century Gothic church was improved and enlarged to its present size. It has a pleasing internal harmony strangely lacking in many of the other churches in Bruges, illuminated by pale pink light when the sun is shining. The interior is decorated with an abundance of 16th- to 18th-century paintings and tombs. The glorious canopied pulpit is worth a closer inspection for its intricate, skillful carving; among the most interesting of the tombs is the two-tiered arrangement of Ferry de Gros and his two wives. De Gros, who died in 1544, was a treasurer of the Order of the Golden Fleece. The tomb, which is decorated with a ceramic tondo, is reminiscent of the Italian Renaissance, with ornate floral designs in the ceramic wall-tiles. Once back outside, Sint-Jakobsstraat leads directly back to the Markt.

TRIPS FROM BRUGES

After the near perfection of Bruges, any other town in the region can seem rather disappointing, but there are several places of interest that you may like to explore on your way to or from the city. Most of them are no more than a few miles from Bruges. The exceptions are the World War I battlefields around Ieper (Ypres)—there are organized coach trips, but you may prefer to drive yourself—and Veurne. For descriptions of Brussels, Antwerp, and Belgium's coastal resorts, see the *Berlitz Pocket Guide to Brussels*.

Tillegembos

Bus number 25 will take you to the woods of Tillegembos in Bruges' southwestern suburb, Sint-Michiels. They cover an area of 81 hectares (200 acres), providing a real rural retreat if you need a break from the city. Lots of well-marked footpaths take you around this former estate, and there is also a lakeside inn and play areas for children. An elegant, moated castle dating from the 14th century is today the headquarters of the West Flanders Tourist Board.

☛ Loppem

Situated just 3 km (2 miles) south of Bruges, the Château at Loppem is a splendid example of Neo-Gothic architecture, originally conceived by August Pugin (architect of the British Houses of Parliament) and later completed by Jean

Béthune. Built between 1858 and 1863, the structure appears from a distance to be a mass of verticals, all eaves and roof and pinnacles, accentuated by its reflection in the lake before it. Inside, the house is sumptuously decorated, the tone dominated by the wood of the ceilings and furniture. It has a private chapel and a wonderful, soaring hall.

Damme

At the right time of year, you can take a paddle-boat canal cruise from Noorwegse Kaai, ride a bus, or cycle or walk alongside the canal to this picturesque village 7 km (4 miles) northeast of Bruges. The attractive approach-roads to the village are lined with pollarded trees, all kinked in exactly the same spot by the prevailing wind that blows across the open countryside. Once the outer port of its larger neighbour, Damme still retains an air of medieval prosperity, boasting-

The Château at Loppem may look forbidding, but inside it is a richly furnished, lovely home.

Damme's charming Stadhuis looks across the marketplace at some fine restaurants.

some fine old buildings and excellent restaurants around its marketplace. With a windmill and skating on the canal in winter, Damme is everyone's idea of a typical Flemish village.

Damme's one main street (Kerkstraat) boasts a delightful **Stadhuis** (town hall) with four corner turrets, built in 1468. Its façade of white sandstone is adorned with the statues of various counts of Flanders, among them Charles the Bold and Margaret of York, and a 15th-century sundial. At one corner, two "stones of justice" hang from the wall. They used to be tied to the neck or feet of unfortunate women who had given offence in some way, and who were then made to parade round the village. Inside the Stadhuis you will find some original, beautifully carved doors. To the right of the building as you face it is **De Grote Sterre** (The Great Star), a twin-gabled 15th-century house that became the home of the Spanish governor in the 17th century. Almost destroyed in a storm in 1990, it has recently undergone extensive restoration. It now houses the Tourist Information Office. Four doors farther down, at number 13, is the 15th-century house where the wedding party of Charles the Bold and Margaret of York was held in 1468. Royal weddings were certainly done in lavish style: in Bruges the celebrations lasted two weeks.

St. Jan's Hospitaal is across the road and down from the Stadhuis. Founded in 1249, it includes a Baroque chapel and a museum of painting, liturgical objects, and sacred books. Farther up the street and visible from the museum is the 13th-century tower of one of Bruges' prominent beacons, the **Onze Lieve Vrouwkerk** (Church of Our Lady). The church has endured many vicissitudes down the centuries, including a fire started in 1578 by soldiers belonging to the Prince of Orange. The tower, gaining its present appearance as a result of partial demolition in 1725, is now the haunt of stray weeds and jackdaws. The separate nave, which has been restored, can be visited in the summer months, when the site seems rather less menacing.

Signposts will lead you to the town's former herring market, which comprises an attractive circle of whitewashed cottages surrounding the village's first drinking-water pump.

Flanders Field

Southwest of Bruges towards the French border with France lies Flanders Field, a vast area of countryside that witnessed a military conflagration on an unprecedented scale. Although the senseless waste of millions of lives in World War I has gone down in history, the staggering numbers killed nevertheless still have the power to appal. Row upon row of gravestones in the many cemeteries of the area testify to the carnage of war. Whether or not you have relatives buried here, the peacefulness of the place and the solidarity in death

The power of wind and water: Damme's prosperity and charm depend on both.

of troops from all sides make for a moving and strangely comforting experience—the soldiers' ordeal is at an end.

There are coach tours available from Bruges that visit selected towns, war cemeteries, and memorials. Alternatively, if you wish to take more time and follow your own inclinations, it is worth taking a car (or even a bicycle) and making use of "Route 14-18," a carefully signposted route through the battlefield area of the Ieper Salient. It should be stressed, however, that nothing much remains of recognizable battlefield. Where you wish to go will depend on any family connections you may have with the war, and what follows is necessarily selective.

Ieper (Ypres) is a name that still resonates in the collective memory. The focus of repeated attacks and counter-attacks, it was shelled to destruction during World War I, then carefully reconstructed over the next 40 years. Nothing old remains in the bustling town, but it has an open, relaxed central Grote Markt and an imposing Stadhuis. The **Salient Museum** in the Stadhuis is worth a visit if you have time—the limitations of the exhibition are overcome by some powerful images of the devastated countryside, and by pitiful mementoes such as banknotes, caps, badges, and buttons. The famous **Menin Gate** memorial, located just off the Grote Markt, is built on a cutting through which thousands of men made their way toward the Ieper Salient. Designed by Reginald Blomfield and comprised of a Classical façade fronting a vast arch with three open ceiling portals, it is inscribed with the names of nearly 55,000 Allied soldiers who died but have no graves.

Just southeast of Ieper, near Zillebecke, **Hill 62** stands as the memorial to the Canadian troops who lost their lives. Near the hill, **Sanctuary Wood Cemetery** preserves a few remaining parts of trenches. At **Hill 60** a little farther beyond Zillebecke, a roadside memorial commemorates the fallen of Australia, behind which lies a field of mounds and hollows, created by intensive bombardment, where you can still make out the ruins of bunkers. This "strategically important" hill was constantly taken and retaken throughout World War I. Today, sheep graze here and birds sing in the trees. A natural memorial—more effective than the official tributes—is a circle of silver birches growing in a pool of water.

A little over 10 km (6 miles) northeast of Ieper, situated off the N332 before Passendale, is **Tyne Cot Military Cemetery.** The largest military cemetery in the world, it was designed by the architect Sir Herbert Baker, who aimed to evoke the appearance of a traditional English graveyard. Its large Cross of Sacrifice in Portland stone is built on the site of the Tyne Cot dressing station that was finally captured by the Austrian troops in 1917. It watches over nearly 12,000 white gravestones standing honourably in regular formation on a green lawn, the unidentified graves simply inscribed: "A soldier of the Great War, known unto God." The cemetery is enclosed at the top by a semi-circular wall bearing the names of 35,000 soldiers who were never found. The slight rise on which the cemetery is located affords a view over the now-peaceful countryside.

The German cemetery located at **Langemark,** approximately 16 km (10 miles) north of Ieper, contains more than 44,000 German soldiers—over half of them in a mass grave.

It is referred to as the Students' Cemetery because so many young soldiers perished at Langemark in 1914 and 1915. The gravestones are simple tablets that lie flush with the lawn, on ground sheltered by mature trees. The cemetery contains the remnants of three bunkers.

Farther northwest, 4 km (2½ miles) outside the town of Diksmuide, **Vladslo** German cemetery is the site of over 25,000 German graves and an extremely moving memorial sculpture by Käthe Kollwitz entitled *Grieving Parents*. The sculptor's son lies buried there.

There are more than 150 war cemeteries in the area. The graves go on and on: Flanders Field belongs to the dead more than the living.

Veurne

A small town (with a population not much greater than that of Damme), just 6 km (4 miles) from the border with France, Veurne grew from a ninth-century fortress and now boasts an attractive central marketplace, among the best in Belgium. The town's Procession of the Penitents takes place on the last Sunday in July, presenting scenes from Christ's Passion. Owing much to Spanish influence (the town once served as a Spanish garrison), the procession is similar to the celebration of "Semana Santa." There are also other processions during Easter and Lent.

Most of Veurne's places of interest are in or alongside the central Grote Markt, where you'll also find plenty of cafés and restaurants. Tickets for guided tours and carriage rides through the town are available in the summer months from the tourist office in the square.

The typical yellow Flemish brick is much in evidence, together with an architectural style that shows the Spanish presence in its restraint. The gabled **Stadhuis** in the Grote

The canal between Bruges and Ghent is still an important artery linking the two towns.

Markt, built in 1612, has an attractive loggia of bluestone contrasting with the yellow brick of the rest of the structure. The building is open to visitors; among its fine interiors are some unusual and impressive leather wall hangings originating from Cordoba in southern Spain.

The **Landhuis,** adjoining the Stadhuis, was built in 1616, its Gothic bell-tower topped with a Baroque spire. Next door is a delightful parade of five houses with step gables, each with a different design of columns around the windows. The cafés on the ground floors spill out into the square on warm days. On the northeast side of the square is the **Spanish Pavilion,** which, as the name suggests, was the headquarters for Spanish officers during the 17th century. Across the road, the building with all the window shutters is the Renaissance **Vleeshuis** (Meat Market), built in 1615, now a library.

The great unfinished tower of **Sint-Niklaaskerk,** rising from nearby Appelmarkt, can be climbed for the view. The 13th-century structure has a carillon. The other church in the town of Veurne is **Sint-Walburgakerk,** of which construction began in 1250 with ambitious plans that eventually proved too much for the little town. It has a splendid 27-metre (90-foot) nave. The interior of the church is worth a visit, more for its overall effect than for any specific item, though there is a fine Baroque pulpit.

GHENT

Ghent, the capital of East Flanders, lies at the confluence of the Scheldt river and the Leie. In contrast to its near neighbour and traditional economic rival, it is a city with more on its mind than just the tourist industry. Though it suffered the same economic decline as Bruges, historically it has been more successful in cultivating new sources of income and

Flowers and other produce on sale at Kouter Square's market attract a lot of business.

wealth, particularly in the 19th century, when the industrialization of the country worked to Ghent's advantage. Today, it is a city built on diverse economic interests, with the sense to preserve its historical heart—a city confident in its future and proud of its past. That past is shown in some magnificent buildings, second only to Bruges in their splendour. Many of them are being renovated and there is still much to do, but the various states of decay and preservation of the old buildings add to the excitement of discovery and one's sense that Ghent is on the move.

The sea-port city has an almost Mediterranean air about it, with cafés and bars spilling out onto the pavements at the slightest hint of warmth. The large student population drawn to Ghent's university makes for a more lively atmosphere than in Bruges. Fortunately for visitors used to the compactness and sheer "walkability" of Bruges, most of Ghent's cultural landmarks are confined within a relatively small area. The walks described below start from St. Baafsplein. Most of Ghent's historic Inner Town lies northwest of this square, straddling the Y-shaped meeting of the two rivers. This area is one of winding streets and alleyways, while the south is lined with elegant boulevards and imposing mansions.

St. Baafsplein

Standing in St. Baafsplein you can see Sint-Baafskathedraal on its east side, the Belfry and Lakenhalle on the west side, and the Royal

A statue of van Artevelde watches over the whole busy scene.

Flemish Theatre on the north. To the south stands a memorial to Jan Frans Willems (1793–1846), who founded the Flemish movement. The oldest theatre in Ghent stood on the site of the **Hof Hamelinck** at number 10, constructed in 1739 (it's the house with the bust of the goddess Juno in its gable).

Sint-Baafskathedraal

The largely Gothic brick-and-granite **Sint-Baafskathedraal** was built over some centuries, the chancel dating from the turn of the 14th century, both the tower and the nave from the 15th century, and the transept from the mid-16th century. This magnificent structure is the first among many churches well worth visiting in Ghent, for itself as well as for the treasures it contains. The airy nave of the cathedral is an invigorating sight for even the most foot-sore visitor. A forest of stone bathed in light leads the eye onward and upward to a

glorious Late-Gothic display of rib vaulting in the roof high above. The tower, providing some splendid views, also contains a carillon, while the crypt retains some of the original structure of an earlier Romanesque church.

The cathedral's (and also the city's—and probably even the nation's) greatest treasure, located in a side chapel to the left of the main

Beauty without: the striking exterior of Sint-Baafskathedraal.

entrance, should on no account be missed. Variously known as the *Ghent Altarpiece* or *The Adoration of the Mystic Lamb,* this marvellous panel painting is regarded as the crowning achievement of Jan van Eyck's Gothic style. Whether or not he actually was responsible for the work has in the past been a matter of some dispute. An inscription on the frame of the altarpiece declares that it was started by Hubert van Eyck and completed by his famous brother Jan. However, since no one has any other evi-

A detail from van Eyck's crowning achievement, the Ghent Altarpiece.

dence for the existence of Hubert, it is thought by many that he was the mythical creation of Ghent citizens jealous of Bruges' monopolizing of Jan. Certainly, it is difficult to believe that an artist of van Eyck's genius could be surpassed by someone who has otherwise left nothing to posterity, and most art historians today unhesitatingly attribute the work of this painting solely to the master artist Jan van Eyck.

Just why is the work so special? To art historian E. H. Gombrich, van Eyck in this painting completed "the final conquest of reality" in the northern Gothic tradition. Van Eyck did not investigate the principles of perspective scientifically like contemporary Italian masters—for example, the keyboard that the angel plays in the inside right-hand panel has almost no depth to it at all. What he did achieve, rather, was the accumulation of so much closely observed detail that he broke completely with medieval ideas and styles and instituted a new kind of realism. The altarpiece seems to become increasingly detailed the closer you look at it. Look closely at his horses and people: they are real creatures of flesh and blood. His flowers and trees are astonishingly accurate; his portraits of the donors on the outside panels look like mercilessly truthful records of living individuals with all their imperfections.

You can see all this detail for yourself. The painting as a whole is invested with a wonderful humanity and optimism, with the God the Father, wise and beneficent, looking kindly upon all. If you look carefully, you will also see Bruges Cathedral depicted in the background of the central panel.

Whether or not you have the strength of mind to leave van Eyck's masterpiece for last or wish to rush to it first, there are many other important works of art to be seen in the cathedral here. Rubens' painting of 1624, *The Conversion of St. Baaf,* in the far left-hand side of the chancel, is full of the unique drama with which the artist infused all his work; it also contains a self-portrait in the red-cloaked convert. Just beyond the transept on the right-hand side of the chancel is Frans

Pourbus' *Christ among the Doctors,* painted in 1571. The youthful Jesus is shown amazing the elders of the temple with his knowledge and wisdom, but it is his audience that claims our attention. Pourbus portrayed in

Ghent's Belfort, over 600 years old, is a symbol of the city's independence.

the crowd contemporary luminaries such as Philip II and Charles V, Thomas Calvin, and even his rival, painter Pieter Breughel the Elder. Down in the crypt is the striking *Calvary Tryptych* of Justus van Gent, painted in 1466 and clearly owing a debt of gratitude to van Eyck in its precise attention to detail.

A stunning view of the city as seen from the majestic 91-metre (298-foot) Belfort.

You will also find splendid examples of sculpture, the best of which is the Baroque oak-and-marble pulpit, one of Laurent Delvaux's masterpieces, completed in 1741. The dynamic, intricate carving of the design sweeps the eye up to where the preacher would stand, above which a marble tree of knowledge grows complete with gilded serpent and fruit. St. Bavo himself is commemorated in the Baroque high altar of sculptor Hendrik Frans Verbruggen.

Belfort and Lakenhalle

Opposite the cathedral, the **Belfort** (Belfry), completed in 1380, has since become the preeminent symbol of the city's independence. From March until November, a vertiginous lift ascent to the top of the 91-metre (298-foot) tower will reward you with spectacular views across the city. The gilded copper dragon at the top of the spire was first installed upon completion of the tower, but the present creature and the four figures poised at the corners of the viewing platform are modern replicas. The spire itself was restored at the beginning of the 20th century according to the original 14th-century design. The impressive workings of the clock and the 52-bell carillon can be closely inspected on the fourth floor of the tower.

On the north side of the Belfort stands the gaolhouse of the former prison, which has above its doorway a carved relief symbolic of Christian charity known as the "Mammelokker." This shows the old man Cimon, who has been condemned to death by starvation, being suckled by his daughter.

Together with the Belfort, the neighbouring **Lakenhalle** (Cloth Hall) magnificently expresses Ghent's civic pride and commercial wealth. The building was much restored in 1903, but dates from 1441, once serving as the meeting place for the city's wool and cloth traders. Sadly, the interior of the building is today relatively empty, though there is a short audio-visual display devoted to Ghent's history.

North of St. Baafsplein

Botermarkt and Hoogpoort

Across the road from the Lakenhalle in Botermarkt stands the rather formidable **Stadhuis** (Town Hall), all pilasters and windows; it was built over a long period and in different styles, but manages to retain a surprising degree of architectural unity. The Stadhuis is like a giant calendar of architecture: the oldest part of the building (on the Hoogpoort side) dates from the early 16th century, and, with its florid design and ornate statues, follows the style of Bruges' Stadhuis. Religious disputes in 1539, associated with the end of the wool trade and economic decline of Ghent, halted the work for some 60 years, so Rombout Keldermans' design (incorporating statues in every conceivable niche and an ornate way with windows) was never completed. Work began again with the Renaissance-style façade of the Botermarkt side of the hall; it was continued in the 18th century with the Baroque façade facing the corner of Hoogpoort and Stadhuissteeg and the Rococo Poeljemarkt side. The Stadhuis provides a historic introduction to the museums of Ghent, as it was from a balcony in this building that the Pacification of Ghent was proclaimed (see page 16). The throne room and an impressive city council room are accessible inside. Guided tours, which are well worth joining, start in April and are available throughout the summer.

North from the Stadhuis and St. Baafsplein, Hoogpoort runs northwest past some beautiful Ghent houses. On the corner with the square stands **Sint-Jorishof,** the former house of the Guild of Crossbowmen (now a hotel), built in 1477. It was in this house that Mary of Burgundy granted a charter of freedoms to the Flemish cloth towns (see page 15). At 10 Hoogpoort is **De Ram.** This house, built in 1732, was formerly home to an apothecary. A lamp (traditional

A visit to Ghent is incomplete without a voyage of discovery along its canals.

emblem of apothecaries) is carved in the façade, as are relief portraits of the botanist, Carolus Clusius. A few doors
down from De Ram, music emanates from Ghent's Royal
Conservatory of Music—during term time, you will see
students carrying a variety of musical instruments around
the streets.

Around Groentenmarkt and Korenmarkt

Hoogpoort will lead you to Groentenmarkt, site of the medieval pillory and former fishmarket. The **Groot Vleeshuis,**
on the west side of the square, comprises a complex of gabled
buildings restored in 1912 but dating from 1406. The buildings include a covered meat market, a guild-house, and a
chapel. Nowadays, visitors are drawn to a variety of cafés,
shops, and stalls which can be found underneath the steeples,
pitched roof, and stepped gables of the renovated market.

Korenmarkt (Cornmarket) connects with the Groentenmarkt; at its southern end stands the landmark of **Sint-
Niklaaskerk** (St. Nicolas' Church), from where Sint-
Michielsbrug (St. Michael's Bridge) spans the Leie River. This
area offers some of the most characteristic views of Ghent; you
can make out the towers of the Belfry and Sint-Baafs, the picturesque Korenlei and Graslei quaysides, and the ominous
mass of Gravensteen castle. Across from the bridge you will
see **Sint-Michielskerk** (St. Michael's Church).

The oldest parts of the Scheldt Gothic Sint-Niklaaskerk
date back to the 13th century, but the building was not completed until the 18th century. Inside, the Baroque high altar is a
typically energetic design of the period. The whole church is
flooded with a beautiful light on sunny days. Various guilds
and "De Fonteyne" (a kind of debating society for those who
fancied themselves as orators) shared a chapel here; their
meeting-house is situated behind the church at Goudenleeuw-

plein 7, built in 1539 in Renaissance style.

Across the Leie River, Sint-Michielskerk acts as a kind of visual balance to Sint-Niklaaskerk; it should be visited for the sake of viewing Anton van Dyck's striking *Crucifixion,* painted in 1629. More famous for his portraits than his religious works, in this painting van Dyck's characteristic melancholy tone is heightened by the subject of Christ's Passion into a scene that is transcendentally sorrowful. Works by de Crayer are also displayed.

Resplendent in sunshine: the High Altar of Sint-Niklaaskerk, bathed in light.

Adjacent to the church in Onderbergen, there is a former Dominican monastery, known as **Het Pand.** The oldest parts of this harmonious complex of buildings—now owned and used by Ghent's university—date back to the 13th century. The monks could not have picked a more agreeable place to live, with the waters of the Leie lapping close by.

Korenlei and Graslei

Looking northward from Sint-Michielsbrug, you'll be eager to stroll on both banks of the river, past a splendid array of medieval guild-houses on the quaysides. Korenlei, on the left, and Graslei, on the right, comprise Ghent's oldest harbour, the **Tussen Bruggen** (Between the Bridges). This was

These guild shields are typical of the fine detailing on Ghent's historic buildings.

the commercial heart of the medieval city and the place where Ghent's guilds chose to build. If you wander about and spend enough time looking, you may be able to pick your favourite house, but the choice is not easy. Along Korenlei, ones to watch out for include: number 7, the 1739 **Gildehuis van de Onvrije Schippers** (House of the Tied Boatmen), which is an excellent example of Flemish Baroque, with spectacular dolphins and lions adorning the gables and a gilded ship crowning the roof; and the 16th-century **De Zwane** (The Swans) at number 9, a former brewery which has a swan charmingly depicted in two *tondi* on the gables.

Look over the water to Graslei for a view of the even finer houses on that quay before crossing for a closer inspection. The **Gildehuis van de Vrije Schippers** (House of the Free Boatmen) was built in 1531, in Brabant Gothic style, while next door, the second Baroque **Gildehuis van de Graanmeters** (House of the Grainweighers) dates back to 1698. (Don't confuse this second grainweighers' house with the first one built up the road in 1435) The little **Tolhuisje** (Customs House), built in 1682, looks like a charming Renaissance afterthought. Next door is the Romanesque-style **Het Spijker,** also known as Koornstapelhuis (a former grain warehouse), dating from about 1200, and on the other side is the Korenmetershuis (Corn Measurer's house, now home to a restaurant), followed by the Gothic **Gildehuis van de Metselaars** (House of the Masons), dating back to 1527 and built in Brabant Gothic style.

North of Korenlei

Jan Breydelstraat branches off from the north end of Korenlei. The **Museum voor Sierkunst** (Museum of Decorative Arts) at number 5 occupies a house built in 1755 by the de Coninck family. Containing rooms decorated in period style, it is devoted to interior design and furnishings up to the 19th century, with a separate wing for modern furniture. Of historical note are pieces once owned by Catherine II of Russia and France's Louis XVIII (the French king, who was understandably nervous about Napoleon, fled to Ghent to avoid him). The older wing contains a memorably ornate carved wooden Rococo chandelier, while a room decorated in Empire style looks the most restful and harmonious. The new wing for modern furniture is an imaginative and exciting conversion of the old building, with internal balconies and gangways designed in an international style — it's rather like being on an ocean liner. Many of the modern items on display are equally innovative, including a curious armchair covered in quilted imitation banana skins.

Farther along, in adjacent Burgstraat, the Renaissance-gabled house decorated with portraits of the Counts of Flanders is the **Huis der Gekroonde Hoofden** (House of the Crowned Heads). From here, Gewad leads into Prinsenhof, which will take you under the **Donkere Poort** (Dark Gate), which is all that remains of the Prinsenhof Palace that was inhabited by Charles V and the Counts of Flanders since 1353. The street ends at **Rabot,** one of the most emblematic places in the city. It was at this lockhouse that the army of Emperor Friedrich III was kept at bay by the citizens of Ghent. The lockhouse, its massive round towers rather at odds with the characteristic stepped gables, was built in 1489. A key element of Ghent's defences was to open the lock to flood the surrounding area, effectively sealing off the city by turning it into an island. The modern tower-blocks will dominate your view of the place, but the renovated lockhouse counts as an important feature on the canal journeys that operate from Graslei.

☞ *Gravensteen*

A quiet footpath along Sint-Antoniuskaai leads to Augustijnenkaai and **Gravensteen,** the heavily renovated island fortress that was once the Castle of the Counts. The castle is still a powerful and ominous presence here, with massive fortifications comprising crenellated cylindrical towers and a vast brooding keep. Work began on the structure in 1180 at the behest of Philip of Alsace, on the site of a ninth-century castle. The building was modelled on the Crusader Castles of the Holy Land; a climb along the battlements (particularly at the top of the keep) provides excellent views and a welcome blast of fresh air. A tunnel leads to the central courtyard, which is surrounded by turreted walls. The central keep may be reached via spiral staircase. Inside, the keep contains the

living quarters of a succession of Counts of Flanders, including the impressive Great Hall where Philip the Good feasted the Knights of the Golden Fleece in 1445. There is also a display of torture equipment (among which you will find a guillotine), which greatly fascinates most children, as well

Gravensteen Castle, once an ominous presence, is now great fun to explore.

as underground dungeons. An easy-to-follow, arrowed route takes the visitor through the complex arrangement of narrow staircases, passages, and chambers.

From Kraanlei to Vrijdagmarkt

Between the castle and Kraanlei is Sint-Veerleplein, where the Inquisition burned its heretics on days when there wasn't a market. The old fish market at number 5 (with Neptune dominating the gateway) was constructed in 1689, in exuberant Baroque style. Kraanlei is lined with various fine houses; at number 65 the almshouses are now home to the **Museum voor Volkskunde** (Museum of Folklore). Founded in 1363, this beautifully restored former children's hospital is comprised of 18 interconnected Flemish cottages arranged around a courtyard. Each room is decorated in the style typical of around 1900. The everyday life of working people is evoked through the items and tools they would have known and used and the few luxuries they could afford. The exten-

---

Ghent in Bloom

The Belgians have long been renowned for their green thumbs, and, as far back as the 16th century, plants were cultivated around Ghent in "orangeries"—ancestors of the modern greenhouse. Ghent's Flower Festival is held every five years in the city's Expo Halls. It's hard to believe that this enormous, sophisticated exhibition originated in 1809, when some 50 plants were displayed in a small inn rearranged for the occasion. Today, hundreds of thousands of visitors admire glorious displays of ornamental flowers, fountains, gardens, and the odd forest, too. Inspired by this abundance, the citizens of Ghent go to Kouter square, which since the 18th century has hosted a flower and bird market every Sunday, to stock up on plants for their own gardens.

---

sive display includes a variety of workshops and stores of the period, plus living and dining rooms.

Some other houses in Kraanlei that will draw your attention include numbers 1–13, built from the 14th to the 15th centuries. The 17th-century house at number 75, called "De Klok," is decorated with allegorical designs representing such virtues as love, faith, and justice. Numbers 77 and 79 are similarly covered.

Crossing the Leie via the Zuivelbrug leads to Grootkannonplein, where you will meet **Mad Meg**—not an eccentric Ghent citizen but a 16-ton cannon made in the 15th century. Standing on the quayside, supported by three stone plinths, it is quite harmless now and probably wasn't all that deadly when it was used, since early cannons were notoriously inaccurate and this one cracked the first time it was fired. Just a few steps away, the **Vrijdagmarkt** (Friday Market) has some excellent examples of guild-houses, with a 19th-century monument to Ghent hero Jacob van Artevelde at its centre. The stylish Art-Nouveau building named **Ons Huis,** built

These whitewashed cottages are now the home of Ghent's Folklore Museum.

in 1900, belonged to the Socialist Workers' Association; it is attractive to look at, though too tall for the square. Older houses include those at numbers 22 and 43–47, built in the 17th and 18th centuries respectively.

It was in this square that the Flemish Counts were sworn in by the citizens of the city. Visible from the square in Koningstraat, the **Koninklijke Vlaamse Academie** is an imposing but rather badly worn Baroque mansion that looms over the entire length of the street.

East of the Vrijdagmark, in a square of its own, stands **Sint-Jakobskerk** (St. James' Church). The oldest church in Ghent, its structure is basically Romanesque, but, like so many others, the church's construction continued over several centuries, finishing in the 15th.

South of Vrijdagmarkt

A stroll from the church and a right turn into Belfortstraat will take you to the Nederpolder and the **Palais Vanden Meersche** at number 1. This house was built in 1547, but its lovely Rococo courtyard (if you can catch a glimpse of it) was added in the 18th century. A total contrast in style is provided by the house opposite at number 2, a 13th-century Romanesque building called **De Kleine Sikkel.**

Turning right at the end of the Nederpolder alongside the canal and Reep, you can see **Geraard de Duivelhof,** the turreted and fortified mansion built for the steward to the Flemish dukes, who was affectionately known as Geraard de Duivel (Gerard the Devil). Once an asylum for the mentally ill, it is now the home of the East Flemish State Archives, which doubtless makes good use of the building's Romanesque crypt.

You can follow the roads down to the confluence of the rivers Scheldt and Leie, crossing by way of Slachthuisbrug to see the ruins of **Sint-Baafsabdij** (St. Bavo's Abbey). The abbey, founded in 630 by St. Amandus, was once the most powerful in Flanders. Destruction, suppression, and rebuilding over the centuries means that today there is nothing much left of it, but parts of a cloister, the octagonal lavatorium (wash house for monks), the chapterhouse, and refectory can still be seen.

South from St. Baafsplein

Some of the museums south of St. Baafsplein may be of interest only to the specialists and devotees, and they go some way to justifying Belgium's reputation for being a nation of collectors. Even the museums that everyone will wish to visit are not arranged as well as they might be, with some of the items randomly displayed and labelled in Flemish only. Despite this deficiency, these latter have some marvellous exhibits that should on no account be missed.

Around Veldstraat

Veldstraat, running south from Sint-Niklaaskerk, is the city's main shopping street, which you will soon realize from the crowds (the street is pedestrianized, but watch out for the trams). Many of the original build-

The first rays of summer sun bring Ghent's cafés out into the streets.

ing exteriors remain. The most historic and certainly the most flamboyant of these is the **Palais D'Hane-Steenhuyse.** The eye-catching Rococo façade of this 18th-century house is matched only by the Classical façade of its garden frontage. Louis XVIII lived in the house briefly as he fled Napoleon; other inhabitants have included the French writer and statesman Talleyrand and the Tsar of Russia. What they would make of the chain-stores opposite their former home is anyone's guess. At number 82, the **Museum Arnold van der Haeghen** is devoted to the library belonging to Nobel Prize-winning writer Maurice Maeterlinck (1862–1949) and Ghent artist Victor Stuyvaert. The house was built in 1741; in 1815 it was home to the Duke of Wellington. It has a charming Chinese salon with silk wallpaper and a number of 18th- and 19th-century interior designs; it also hosts a variety of temporary exhibitions.

If you turn left at Zonnestraat to **Kouter,** you will find yourself in a square that has good claim to be the most historically significant in the city. A variety of festivals, military parades, meetings, and tournaments have taken place here through the centuries, and flower festivals have been held on Sundays since the 18th century (when it seems every tenth citizen can be seen carrying a small tree). It may be hard to envisage all the pomp of the past, as few buildings of any antiquity have survived, except for the house at number 29 and the former Royal Opera House, just off the square in Schouwburgstraat, which was completed in 1840.

Bijloke Museum

Where Schouwburgstraat rejoins Veldstraat, turn into the Nederkouter, which continues to parallel the Leie. Cross over where the signpost points the way to the **Bijloke Museum.** Perhaps one of the main attractions of this museum is

The Bijloke Museum is dotted with oddities and surprises, such as this ship in full sail.

the building itself, which comprises a series of brick structures from the 14th to 17th centuries that once formed the Cistercian convent of Bijloke. Arranged around a peaceful cloister, it is devoted to the arts of the Ghent region. Despite a slightly flea-market approach to the organization of its exhibits, it is well worth visiting for the interiors. Chief among these is the outstanding 14th-century refectory, painted in a warm terracotta, with a barrel-vaulted ceiling that measures over 31 metres (100 feet) long and 14 metres (45 feet) high. The frescoes that grace this room were painted in 1325 by an unknown master and include a faded but still beautiful *Last Supper.* Somewhat incongruously, the tomb of a 12th-century knight lies in the centre of the room. The Guild Hall, the original dormitory to the convent, is decked with splendid processional regalia of the Ghent guilds—banners, coats of arms, and big ornamental lanterns, plus a model of a ship in full sail.

Museum voor Schone Kunsten

A five- or ten-minute walk along Charles de Kerchovelaan leads to **Citadelpark.** In the eastern corner of the park (conveniently situated opposite the casino, if you're in the mood for a flutter) is the **Museum voor Schone Kunsten** (Museum of Fine Arts), which incorporates the **Museum van Hedendaagse Kunst** (Museum of Contemporary Art). Like the Bijloke Museum, the organization of exhibits leaves something to be desired, but again, there are several very fine items on display. Bosch is represented by *Christ Carrying the Cross,* an unforgettable painting showing Christ on the way to Calvary. The artist emphasizes the characters accompanying Jesus—a procession of grotesques. Even St. Veronica, holding the cloth she used to wipe Christ's brow (which now miraculously bears his image), seems more intent on her memento than the significance of the event itself. An earlier work, less characteristic of the artist, is *St. Jerome at Prayer,* which also features the lion, a symbol of the saint and his conventional companion in portraits through the centuries. Good and evil are represented pictorially by different landscapes in the foreground and background.

Among other Flemish and Dutch exhibits are works by Jacob Jordaens, Frans Hals' bravura *Old Lady*—full of the artist's exuberant brushwork—and Pieter Brueghel the Younger's *Peasant Wedding* and a rather harassed *Village Advocate.* Rubens is represented by a *Scourging of Christ* (worth comparing with Lucas Cranach's painting on the same theme) and *St. Francis Receiving the Stigmata.* Later paintings include Géricault's *Portrait of a Kleptomaniac* and works by Corot, Courbet, Daumier, Ensor, and Rouault. The

Ghent Museums

Bijloke Museum: *Godshuizenlaan 2*. Ghent art and furnishings in a former convent. Open Tuesday–Sunday 9:30am–5pm. BF100. (See page 73)

Gravensteen Castle: *Sint-Veerleplein*. Exciting castle with battlements and museum. Open April–September 9am–6pm; October–March 9am–5pm. BF80. (See page 68)

Museum Arnold van der Haeghen: *Veldstraat 82*. Nobel Prize-winning writer Maurice Maeterlinck's library; temporary exhibitions. Open Tuesday–Sunday 9:30am–5pm. Free. (See page 73)

Museum voor Industriele Archeologie en Textiel (Industrial Archaeology and Textiles): *Minnemeers 9*. All things industrial, in a former textile mill. Tuesday–Sunday 9:30am–5pm. Free.

Museum voor Schone Kunsten (Fine Arts): *Citadelpark*. Paintings from 14th century to present, with masterpieces by Bosch, Brueghel, Hals, and Jordaens. The Museum van Hedendaagse Kunst (Contemporary Art) is also here. Open Tuesday–Sunday 9:30am–5pm. BF100. (See page 75)

Museum voor Sierkunst (Decorative Arts): *Jan Breydelstraat 5*. Period-furnished rooms and contemporary design in superb settings. Open Tuesday–Sunday 9:30am–5pm. BF100. (See page 67)

Museum voor Volkskunde (Folklore): *Kraanlei 65*. Almshouses showing working-class life circa 1900, plus children's puppet theatre. Open April–October 9–12:30am, 1:30– 5:30pm; November–March 10am–noon, 1:30–5pm. Closed Monday. BF80. (See page 69)

Schoolmuseum Michel Thiery: *Sint-Pietersplein 14*. Exhibition of animals, evolution, minerals, computers, and a wonderful complex of buildings. Open Monday–Saturday (except Friday pm) 9–12:15am, 1:30–5:15pm. BF80. (See page 77)

Sint-Martens-Latem artists (whose "colony" was near Ghent) are also represented.

The museum has only a few sculptures, but there is a bust by Rodin and an enticingly erotic bronze by Camille Claudel.

Formerly located in the same building, the Museum van Hedendaagse Kunst is mainly devoted to Belgian paintings made since 1945, with works on display by

"Christ Carrying the Cross," by Bosch, is housed in the Museum of Fine Arts.

Magritte and Karel Appel. In 1999 this will move across the road, allowing for a reorganization of the Museum voor Schone Kunsten.

Sint-Pietersplein

Northward from the museum, Overpoortstraat leads to Sint-Pietersplein, where the **Centrum voor Kunst en Kultur** has regular exhibitions of art and hosts other cultural events. Next door, the **Schoolmuseum Michel Thiery** contains an eclectic mix of exhibits that relate to science taught in schools: fossils and stuffed animals sit cheek by jowl with minerals and model dinosaurs. The highly attractive museum building and courtyard (formerly the infirmary of the Abbey of St. Peter) have recently been fully restored, as was the adjoining church. The splendid 57-metre (188-foot) cupola of **Onze-Lieuve-Vrouw Sint-Pieterskerk** (Church of Our Lady of St. Peter) can be seen for many streets around. The Baroque church was designed by the Huyssens brothers and built in 1719. Clearly, the architects were not lacking in ambition: the design is based on St. Peter's Basilica in Rome. The impressive façade dominates the attractive Sint-Pieter-splein; the church has an exuberant Baroque-style interior and artworks by van Dyck.

From St. Pietersplein, Sint-Kwintensberg leads to Nederkouter, and then Veldstraat.

TRIPS FROM GHENT

Ghent's central location, proximity to the capital, and extensive road and rail connections make it easy to get out and about to other places of interest. Most of those described here are no more than a few miles from the centre of the city. For descriptions of Brussels, Antwerp, and Belgium's coastal resorts, see the *Berlitz Pocket Guide to Brussels*.

☛ Laarne Castle

Some 13 km (8 miles) east of Ghent, served by bus 688 from St. Pieters Station, Laarne Castle is one of the best-preserved medieval moated fortresses in Belgium. Built in a pentagonal design in the 12th century as a defensive fortress for Ghent, it was added to in the 17th century. Its towers with steeply pitched turrets look made for a fairy-tale princess, while the remainder of the building, with its regularly-spaced, mullioned windows, has the air of a substantial but comfortable manor house. A multi-arched bridge leads to a keep, beyond which are two central courtyards.

The rooms' furnishings are really magnificent, with most of the interiors in French and Antwerp style. There is splendid vaulting in the ground-floor hall and many exquisite chimney-pieces. The most important furnishings are also the most lovely—16th-century Brussels tapestries portraying the Emperor Maximilian on a hunt. There is also a gorgeous collection of French and Belgian silver from the 15th to 18th centuries.

The treasures of Laarne Castle are well guarded within their moated fortress.

Oidonk Castle

A little farther southwest of Deurle, 12 km (8 miles) from Ghent, Oidonk is situated in superbly manicured gardens in a bend of the Leie River near the village of Bachte-Maria-Leerne. This startling château, with its Spanish-Flemish style of architecture, brings to mind St. Basil's Cathedral in Moscow. A 16th-century building modernized in the 19th, it stands almost as it did in 1595. A ground-floor porticoed façade is echoed in a first-floor loggia, in turn surmounted by crow-stepped gables, steeply-pitched roofs, turrets, chimneys, and domed balconies. The moat's water laps around the massive circular towers. Although the castle is still inhabited by the Baron de Nevele, a splendid suite of apartments is open to visitors. There is also a tavern, and the grounds of the castle extend into wooded parkland.

Sint Martens-Latem and Deurle

These two villages on the banks of the Leie are respectively 8 km (5 miles) and 12 km (8 miles) southwest of Ghent. Both villages are picturesque in themselves, but are known chiefly for their connection with the Sint-Martens-Latem group of painters. There were strictly two groups: one which formed around the sculptor George Minne in 1897, and an Expressionist group which formed in the 1920s after the interruption of World War I. The galleries and even the church in Sint Martens-Latem have many of this second group's paintings on show.

Deurle has three museums devoted to the work of Gust de Smet, his brother Leon de Smet, and to Flemish Expressionism as a whole.

Oudenaarde

Only a 28-minute train ride from Ghent, the small town of Oudenaarde lies on the banks of the Schelde River, 30 km (20 miles) to the south. Once famous for its thriving tapestry weaving industry, since the 18th century the town has, for the most part, fallen asleep economically. You can find a few restaurants in Stationsstraat, Hoogstraat, and the Markt.

Undoubtedly, Oudenaarde's glory is the **Stadhuis,** located in the expansive Markt in the town centre. Designed by Brussels architect Henry van Pede, this 16th-century Late-Gothic confection is his masterpiece. Dwarfing the buildings on the perimeter of the square, the town hall's yellow sandstone façade is comprised of a Gothic-arched portico, followed by two tiers of nobly-proportioned windows, and topped with a wedding-cake of a roof. The interior is open to visitors in the summer months.

In the square in front of the Stadhuis, the fountain of frolicking dolphins was financed by Louis XIV in 1671. Behind the Stadhuis is the 13th-century **Lakenhalle** (Cloth Hall).

Sint-Walburgakerk in the Markt has an immediately recognizable leaning lantern-topped tower. Behind it is the **Notre Dame Hospital,** originally founded in the 12th cen-

The hybrid design of the splendid Oidonk Castle is both whimsical and impressive.

tury outside the town walls. There is a 13th-century chapel, while the main building dates from the 18th century. The Bishop's residence, dating from around 1600, is generally considered one of the finest Renaissance buildings in the country.

You can stroll past the houses opposite the church and into the Burg, past the **Bejinhof** with its Renaissance archway. The Burg becomes Kasteelstraat before ending at the Schelde. Across the river, the **Church of Notre Dame of Pamele** is an early Gothic design of the 13th century. Up the road on the far side of the Tussenbruggen is the **Huis de Lalaing,** a pretty 1717 Rococo house which has a museum and a workshop devoted to tapestries and their restoration, together with an exhibition of work by Oudenaarde artists. (The museum and exhibition at Huis de Lalaing are likely to change location periodically while the restoration of various buildings continues.)

On the other side of the Markt in Hoogstraat, the magnificent façades of the **Episcopal College** date from the 16th and 18th centuries.

WHAT TO DO

SHOPPING

The thought of shopping in Bruges or Ghent may not immediately leap to mind, but both cities have an excellent range of stores of all descriptions. Bruges is more adapted to the lucrative tourist trade than is Ghent; you'll find more in the way of specialized stores and souvenirs. However, Ghent has the bigger shopping centre, with more of a "city" ambience to it. Except for certain items, such as beer bought at the supermarket and chocolates, prices are probably what you would expect to pay at home.

Shopping Hours

General shopping hours are from 9:00 or 9:30 A.M. to 5:30 or 6:00 P.M., with many of the small stores closing for an hour at lunchtime. Late-night shopping tends to be on Fridays, when many stores will remain open until 7:00 or 7:30 P.M. All stores are closed on Sunday, except for the most determined of food kiosks.

Where to Shop

In Bruges, the main shopping street is Steenstraat, off the Markt, which has everything you would expect in the way of stores catering to everyday local needs, including clothes, shoes, food, home furnishings, and electrical goods. There are also a few stores that sell Belgian chocolates and other souvenirs. As can be expected, the street and its associated malls become very crowded on Saturdays, when the best time to go is first thing in the morning.

Bruges' network of small city-centre streets and alleys conceals a surprising number of stores, most of them specializing in items such as lace, chocolate, or clothing. Particular streets to look at are those immediately surrounding the Burg and the Markt. Most of the city's squares have very few shops: the Markt and the Burg are bounded by historical buildings with some cafés and restaurants; Jan van Eyckplein has none; and 't Zand is all bistros and hotels. The exception is Sint-Janplein, home of Bruges' theatre, where there are stores and one small arcade, the Theaterboetieks.

In Ghent, the main shopping street is Veldstraat, which is pedestrianized except for the trams, so do be careful and keep a listening ear out for the tram bell. The shops along this street are mostly for local consumption, but the streets and alleys leading off it conceal excellent specialist stores, as do Korte Meer, Voldersstraat, and Niklaasstraat (parallel to Veldstraat). A modern shopping street (Lange Munt) links Hoogpoort with the Vrijdagmarkt, which itself has only a few stores.

Tax-free shopping is available in stores that display the appropriate notice—usually the larger or more expensive

You may find a bargain at Ghent's flea market, though it's best to get there early.

specialized stores. If you're not sure, ask for details in the shop (see also page 121).

Good Buys

Antiques: These are plentiful in both Bruges and Ghent, sold mostly in small, intimidatingly expensive-looking stores in the narrow, quiet side-streets off the main shopping areas.

Beer: A "must buy" if you have developed a taste for it, as it may not be available for love nor money at home. You will need a car to carry significant quantities.

It's easy to throw restraint to the wind when you enter one of the chocolatiers.

The range is vast, of course, so it will make sense to buy those you have tried and liked rather than risk being disappointed by an unknown. It is much cheaper to buy beer at a conventional supermarket, but they may not stock your favourites. A good place to try in Bruges is the Delicatessen Deldycke at Wollestraat 23, which stocks "The Pride of Bruges" and 12-bottle selection crates. In Ghent, the small shop in Het Spijker building in Graslei provides presentation packs of a number of beers. You can buy Grain Genever (the gin speciality of Ghent) at Bruggeman, Wiedauwkaai 56.

Chocolate: "Made in Belgium," undoubtedly the best in the world, is available everywhere. It's best to avoid the tourist-oriented products, such as the chocolate rabbits and the life-size chocolate breasts, and concentrate on the incomparable delights of the classic, exquisite, hand-made Belgian praline and truffle. Selection boxes (pre-packed, or filled with your own choices) can be bought in a range of weights and are always gift-wrapped attractively. Prices vary enormously, with hotel-foyer stock the worst value for your money. A good shop to visit in Bruges is van Oost at Wollestraat 9, a small store with a select range, while in Ghent, the Leonidas store in Veldstraat offers an extensive range at very reasonable prices. More exclusive and very much more expensive is the Godiva Chocolatier in Voldersstraat, which has a marvellous selection of beautifully presented and finely crafted chocolates. Bear in mind that all these sweets are made with fresh ingredients, so it's therefore essential that they are eaten promptly.

Food and wine: Purchases may be limited by your appetite, the freshness of the produce, or even the size of your car, but it would be a shame not to come away with something, even if it is just for your return journey. Belgium is justly celebrated for its pâtisseries and cakes, and there are some superb specialist food stores and delicatessens in both Bruges and Ghent. Bruges is particularly well served: the Bakerij Sint Paulus in the Theaterboetieks arcade has (as well as chocolates) excellent fruit breads, coffees, and fabulous cakes—the place bustles on Sundays. The Nicolas Pâtisserie at Vlamingstraat 14 has an equally delectable selection, while the aforementioned Delicatessen Deldycke at Wollestraat 23 has an excellent range of fine foods and wines. De Kaaskelder at 40 Genthof has racks of wine as well as gargantuan cheeses from all over.

In Ghent, mustard made in the city can be bought from Tierenteyn at Groentenmarkt 3, and some delicious farm-made cheeses are available from Het Hinkelspel at F. Lousbergkaai 23.

Household furnishings: Not often associated with Belgium, but you may be surprised by the quality and styling of its household goods and furniture, which compare favourably with some of the Scandinavian designs. You can investigate for yourself in Bruges at Callebert at Markt 6, and in Ghent at Frank de Clercq in Oudburg, both of which stock Belgian and overseas designs.

Lace: Found everywhere in Bruges, but beware of imitations. Belgian hand-made lace is expensive, but if you like lace this is the only sort worth buying. It should always be clearly labelled. Breidelstraat (connecting the Markt with the Burg) is the city's lace alley, but it really is sold throughout the city, so you'll have plenty of choice. Reliable sources of guaranteed, authentic Belgian hand-made lace are the family-run Lace Jewel at Philipstockstraat 10-11 and Melissa at Katelijnestraat 38.

Lace is much less in evidence in Ghent, but a good, reliable source is Kloskanthuis at Korenlei 3.

ENTERTAINMENT

Walking, watching, eating, and drinking are the chief pleasures of Bruges and Ghent, but you can tour the cities by boat and by horse-drawn cab—peaceful and relaxing ways to see the sights (see page 116).

Café society is different in the two cities. Bruges' is more interior (although outside tables do appear briefly in the summer), since space and city preservation rules allow little else. In Ghent, given the right weather, outside eating is *de rigueur* and there is more scope for *flânerie* and evening promenading. Belgium's "beer culture" is polite, knowledgeable, and often family-oriented (it's unlikely that you'll come across anything other than the odd burst of the most good-natured high spirits), so it's quite safe for visitors to enjoy.

Bicycles are easy to hire (see page 106) and the cities are flat, though in Bruges you will have to cope with the cobbles and in Ghent with the tram rails. In Bruges, you can cycle to Damme along the canal, while in Ghent you may like to visit the sights and museums just outside the centre.

Nightlife

Music, **opera**, **theatre:** There are regular music festivals and concerts throughout the year in both cities: the city tourist offices will have the latest information. In Ghent, the Flemish Opera in Schouwburgstraat 3 is the most important concert and theatre address. The pleasant Theater Tinnenpot at Tinnenpotstraat 21 stages more avant-garde productions. Hotels and churches in both cities frequently host a variety of concerts and recitals.

Jazz, **folk**, **rock:** With its student population, Ghent is better served than Bruges, which tends to be quiet at night. The Cactus Club at Sint-Jakobsstraat 33 in Bruges is one of the most adventurous venues, with its electro-industrial and frontline-assembly bands, as well as nostalgia events like rock-and-roll dances. In Ghent, a few desultory bars feature canned rock music, but the best place to go is the university area around Sint-

Good beer and good company: the secret of a great night out in Belgium.

Calendar of Events

For the most up-to-date information on the city's festivals and arts calendar, consult the cities' tourist offices. The following list gives an idea of some of the major events.

March   *Bruges*: Film Festival, held at various venues.

April   *Ghent*: Flower Festival, a magnificent international show at Flanders Expo centre (next one will be held in 2000).

May   *Bruges*: Ascension Day Procession of the Holy Blood; historical and ecclesiastical pageant. *Dwars door Brugge*, road race.

May–June   *Ghent*: International Jazz Festival, staged at a variety of venues.

July–August   *Bruges*: Zandfeesten, largest flea market in Flanders (held on Sundays).

July   *Ghent*: Ghent Festival; music and cultural festivities in the city centre.

August   *Bruges*: Festival of the Canals; nocturnal pageant along the illuminated canals. Early Music Festival, various venues. Pageant of the Golden Tree; commemoration once every five years of the wedding of Charles the Bold and Margaret of York (next one to be held in 2001).

Ghent: Patersholfeesten; various festivities in the Het Patershol area of the city. International Chamber Music Festival at various venues.

September   *Ghent*: Flanders Festival; Ghent's share of the music festival, various venues.

October   *Ghent*: International Film Festival.

November   *Bruges*: International Antiques Fair.

December   *Bruges*: Kerstmarkten, Christmas markets, Markt, and Simon Stevinplein.

Pietersplein and on Overpoortstraat, where, at night, there is much more going on. The Sofitel hotel (see page 135) has a jazz bar. The Lazy River Jazz Club in Stadhuissteeg 5 has live jazz every Friday evening, while the Damberd Jazzcafé in Korenmarkt 19 offers live jazz every Tuesday. Blues music (of which the Belgians seem fond) can crop up anywhere.

Cinemas: International films are very often shown in their original language and accompanied by subtitles. In Bruges, the weekly programmes are displayed in the tourist office; otherwise you can try the Kennedy or Chaplin in Zilverstraat and the van Eyck in Smedenstraat. Ghent's most central cinema is the Sphinx in Sint-Michielshelling, but there is also the Decascoop in Ter Platen and the Studio Skoop in Sint-Annaplein.

Nightclubs and discos: There are virtually none and the few that do exist are not worth searching out unless you are truly desperate. In Ghent, most are to be found in the Zuid Quarter.

At home: Any invitation to a meal at a Belgian home is likely to involve extreme hospitality, with copious quantities of food and drink.

SPORTS

Switch on any hotel television and you'll soon learn that football (soccer) is the top spectator sport (Bruges has its own soccer team, good enough to compete in Europe), while cycling and skating are also popular. In Bruges, information about all aspects of recreation can be supplied by Stedelijke Dienst Sport-Recreatie, tel. (050) 44 83 22, while in Ghent you can get information from Dienst Sport en Recreatie, Zuiderlaan 5, tel. (09) 243 88 90. In both cities, you will find all sports facilities in the suburbs. In Bruges, there are swimming pools in St. Kruis and St. Andries, while Ghent has a vast sports centre in Zuiderlaan 5, the Centre Blaarmeersen, offering a variety of recreational activities for families, including windsurfing, fishing, squash, tennis, and athletics facilities, as well as a campsite.

BRUGES AND GHENT FOR CHILDREN

Amusement parks: Boudewijnpark at A. De Baeckestraat 12, Bruges, comprises a dolphinarium with daily shows throughout the year, plus a "Holiday on Ice" show and Bambinoland, "a paradise for the little ones": tel. (050) 38 38 38. In Ghent, the Centre Blaarmeersen offers extensive footpaths and recreational facilities for families: tel. (09) 243 88 70.

Museums and attractions: Most museums will only begin to appeal to older children, but there are some exceptions. If they have a head for heights, then children will love climbing the Belfries in both cities. Gravensteen Castle in

Cyclists pass over lovely tree-lined trails on their way into town.

Ghent has lots of exciting towers, spiral staircases, battlements, and dungeons, and there are gruesome exhibits in the castle's torture museum. The Michel Thiery Museum in Ghent has dinosaur pictures and stuffed animals and fossils, as well as fluorescent minerals on display, and, perhaps more importantly, lots of children looking at them.

A local looks on with a grin: there's plenty to please children in Bruges and Ghent.

Puppet theatre: For younger children, the traditional puppet theatre is bound to enthuse. In Ghent, the puppet theatre in the attic of the Folklore Museum occasionally holds performances. In both cities, tourist information offices have details of venues.

Tours: Children like nothing better than going on the water, and both cities have extensive canals that can be toured by boat. In the summer a large paddle-boat plies between Bruges and Damme. There are also stately horse-drawn carriage rides through Bruges and Ghent, and illuminated buildings lend excitement to evening strolls. You can hire bicycles of different sizes to suit the whole family and explore at the children's pace, or go on a coach tour of the surrounding countryside (see page 116). In Bruges, Cinecitta Hall at Diksmuidestraat 5 has fun, exciting games for children; open on Wednesdays, Saturdays, Sundays, and during school holidays.

EATING OUT

Belgians take their eating very seriously. Their haute cuisine is world-famous, but all their food is of excellent quality. Portions are very generous indeed; even if you ask for a sandwich, your plate will generally arrive loaded with much more than just garnish. Regional cuisines are strongly defined, but in the cities you should have no trouble sampling anything you wish.

Restaurants and Bars

Bruges and Ghent have a great many restaurants, cafés, and bars from which to choose. The word "restaurant" can mean anything from a formal, top-class establishment to a small café. Bars usually serve simple but hearty food at very reasonable prices. Even in the smallest establishment you'll be

served at your table, so, if in doubt, simply take your seat: many restaurant staff speak English and/or French as their second languages. Menus are often printed in a variety of languages, and at lunch (*middagmaal*) and dinner (*avondeten*) there is frequently a tourist menu and a choice of set menus at fixed prices; these represent the best value. Be aware that

Enter a bar and it's possible you'll have over 100 kinds of beer to choose from.

some set meals are served only at lunchtime or only on particular days.

Bars and cafés usually serve snacks in the morning and then lunches from around noon—times are posted in the window along with the menu. Many bars stay open until the early hours of the morning.

Sales and service tax are always included in the bill, so there is no need to tip unless you want to—it certainly will not be expected.

Breakfast

Hotels serve substantial buffet breakfasts (*ontbijt*) which can see you through until lunchtime with no trouble at all. Along with tea or coffee and fruit juice, there will be a variety of breads, cheeses, and meats, plus fresh fruit and cereal, yogurt and fruit salads, buns, and pastries. You may be asked if you would like a boiled egg, and some hotels also provide buffet grills, so you can have a fried breakfast as well. Even in the smaller hotels the choice is usually large and the food very fresh.

Cold Dishes

A *boterham* is an open sandwich, which you'll find served all over the place. Usually comprising two or three huge slices of bread with the filling of your choice plus a salad, they are excellent accompanied by a Belgian beer—and offer great value. There is an enormous range, from salmon to meat to cheeses.

Fish and Shellfish

The close proximity of the North Sea and the traditional culture built around canal and river mean that fish dominates most menus. Alas, the canals of Ghent in particular are now virtually lifeless, but freshwater fish are brought to the table from farther afield.

One great favourite is fresh mussels in season, which are advertised everywhere when they are available, in late winter and early spring. Served simply with wedges of lemon, cooked in butter or cream, they are considered a great delicacy and frequently arrive in a large pan from which diners help themselves. Mussels are often served with that other great Belgian staple, *frites* (chips), particularly at lunchtime.

Trout (*forel*) is another firm favourite, often served in a sauce of white wine, and eel (*aal* or *paling*) crops up a lot, often in thick sauces with herbs: "green eel" is boiled eel with green herbs. Sole (*zeetong*) is served grilled, whilst oysters, lobsters, and crab are dressed in a variety of sauces. Many restaurants have a tank of lobsters or crab on view to entice customers and prove the freshness of the dish. Fish can also feature in the traditional and ubiquitous *waterzooi*,

a stew with vegetables and either fish or chicken; *waterzooi op Gentse wijse* (made with fish) originated in Ghent.

Meat and Poultry

Game, pork, and beef play a prominent part in the Flemish diet, alongside chicken dishes such as *waterzooi*. *Carbonnade* may refer to beef or

The myriad ingredients of **waterzooi,** *a traditional Belgian dish.*

pork cooked in tomato sauce or in a casserole of beer, onions, and herbs. There are also honest-to-goodness beef steaks served with *frites*. Rabbit or hare may be cooked in Gueuze beer with onions and prunes (*konijn met pruimen*), and there are rich pheasant dishes in thick sauces. You may come across goose (*gans*), boiled and then roasted. Veal (*kalf*) and liver (*lever*) dishes are also widely available. *Wildzwijn* looks as if it should mean swan, but rest assured: it is wild boar.

A chef in the process of preparing Belgian cuisine.

Vegetables and Salads

You will find *witlof* on most menus; it is a popular blend of chicory with ham-and-cheese sauce. Other prominent vegetables include Brussels sprouts (*spruitjes*), spinach (*spinazie*), and cauliflower (*bloemkool*).

With all that hot meat and fish around, it is not surprising that salads (*sla, salade*) hardly get a look in, but ones you will find are the *Liège*, which has a mixture of beans and potatoes, and the *wallonie*, which features a combination of potato and bacon. Salads invariably accompany sandwiches.

Cheese

The number of cheeses (*kaas*) is enormous, most of them Belgian, Dutch, or French. Belgium alone produces 300, including

Beers the Belgians Brew

Beer was traditionally popular in Belgium because drinking-water was of such poor quality—the brewing process meant that impurities in the water were rendered harmless. Nowadays, there is nothing to fear from the water—beer is drunk simply because it tastes so good. Enter any bar in Bruges or Ghent for a beer and you may be faced with a choice of 100 or more. Beer is to the Belgians what wine is to the French and, indeed, many Belgian beers complete the last stage of their fermentation in corked champagne bottles. Several hundred different sorts are produced, all of which have their distinctive character and are served in their own type of glass, often accompanied by a dish of cheese or nuts. Consequently, running a bar or café can be a complicated business.

Lambic beers are wild beers, so called because their fermentation involves exposure to wild yeast. Many of them have a sour, apple-like taste, but these may have added fruit to impart the distinctive, thirst-quenching flavour: *Kriek*, a delicious cherry beer, comes in a round glass (served hot if you wish to warm up), while *Frambozen* beer is a pale pink raspberry brew served in a tall wine glass.

White beers are cloudy and are brewed with malt or barley and wheat: they are generally light and youthful in flavour, like the *Brugse Triple* drunk in Bruges.

The label *Trappist* refers to a large number of beers originally brewed in monasteries: *Triple* denotes a very strong beer that was served to the abbot and other important personages; the monks drank the *Dubbel*, while the peasants (namely everyone else) had only a watery version. *Trappist Leffe* is a strong, dark beer, like Porter, slightly sweet and served in a bulbous glass.

Kwak (a strong, blond beer) is served in a glass with a spherical base that sits in a wooden stand in order to remain upright. The 1½-litre glass (about 45 cm/18 inches tall) and its stand are so valuable that customers must often give up a shoe to ensure they don't run off with the merchandise. The design of the Kwak glass is such that towards the end of the drink your beer will suddenly shoot down your throat, so beware.

One of the strongest beers is the appropriately named *Delirium Tremens*, which can really take you by surprise if you're not used to it—though if you see any pink elephants, they really are on the label and not in your head. Another strong beer is *Corsendonck Agnus Dei*, delicious but powerful.

Other terms and types of beer you will come across are *Gueuze*, which is an extremely quaffable, honey-coloured, sweet beer served in a straight glass; *Loburg*, a Brussels-brewed blond beer served in something like a vase; *Hoegaarden Grand Cru*, a refreshing, coriander-based blond beer; *Rodenbach Grand Cru*, a red beer with a sharp apple taste; and *Bourgogne des Flandres*, a light, flavoursome red beer.

Essential bars to visit are (in Bruges) the *'t Brugs Beertje* in Kemelstraat 5, where the friendly and knowledgeable landlord will advise you on all aspects of his 300 or so beers; *De Garre*, in the alley of the same name off Breidelstraat, which has a comfortable ambience and an impressive range of beers that includes its own brand; and (in Ghent) the *Het Waterhuis aan de Bierkant*, Groentenmarkt 9, a popular canal-side bar with more than 100 beers; *De Witte Leeuw*, Graslei 6, a friendly bar with over 100 beers; and *De Dulle Griet*, Vrijdagmarkt 50, which has more than 250 sorts of beer, plus 1½-litre Kwak glasses on proud display and a shoe basket suspended high in the ceiling.

Trappist cheeses such as Orval and Chimay. Belgian Gouda and Remoudou are some of the more well-known names that you may recognize. Meals traditionally end with cheese, so it is wise to leave some room for them if they are on the menu.

Desserts and Pâtisseries

The Belgians love a good dessert, and the more chocolate and cream it has the better. *Ijs* (ice-cream) and *slagroom* (whipped cream) are usually involved somewhere, perhaps oozing from pancakes or waffles. The selection of cakes, fruit tartlets, pastries, buns, and biscuits is immense.

Snacks

Fish and chips are the staple snack of both cities, sold from stalls and vans dotted around the streets. Chips are served in a number of portion sizes and can be topped with ketchup, mayonnaise, mustard, peanut butter sauce—you name it. They are often quite salty, so you may need a drink to accompany them.

There are fast-food places around town—in Bruges, they can be found mostly around the Markt, 't Zand, and Steenstraat, and in

Fruit fresh from the market is an alternative to heady, creamy Belgian desserts.

Ghent you will see them in the Vrijdagmarkt and the Veld-straat area.

Bars serve light snacks such as Croque Monsieur and Toast Cannibal, plus an excellent range of open sandwiches and filled rolls (*belegde broodje*).

Drinks

Some of Belgium's marvellous beers (*bier*) are described on pages 96–97. Most bars will stock at least 20 or 30, and a few will have more than 100. Those on tap (*van 't vat*) are cheaper than the bottled kind. All the usual spirits are available, plus plenty of bottled water. *Genever* is the famous indigenous gin, and it is very strong. Most of the wine (*wijn*) is imported and comes mainly from France and Germany.

Coffee (*koffie*) is fairly strong and usually served with extras such as little biscuits, chocolates, or cake, plus two or three kinds of sugar. Coffee liqueurs (especially Irish coffee) are popular and available everywhere. Tea (*thee*) is often served in a glass with lemon and without milk.

Vegetarians

Although the Belgian diet is dominated by fish and meat, it is easy to adhere to a varied vegetarian regime in Bruges and Ghent. However, this usually means foregoing traditional Flemish cooking. Listed in the Hotels and Restaurants section (see page 129) are a number of places that serve vegetarian food. Be sure not to confuse vegetarian with *vleesgerecht,* which is a meat dish, and remember also that the Belgian chip is likely to have been cooked in animal fat. Some "vegetarian" restaurants also serve meat and fish. If you cannot find a specialty eating house, head for one of the many Italian restaurants—non-meat pasta dishes and salads are usually offered as a matter of course.

To Help You Order ...

I'd like a/an/some ...		**Heeft u ...**	
beer	**bier**	potatoes	**aardappelen**
bread	**brood**	salad	**sla, salade**
coffee	**koffie**	salt	**zout**
dessert	**nagerecht**	soup	**soep**
fish	**vis**	sugar	**suiker**
ice-cream	**ijs**	tea	**thee**
meat	**vleesgerecht**	vegetables	**groente**
milk	**melk**	water	**water**
pepper	**peper**	wine	**wijn**

... And Read the Menu

aardbei	strawberry	**mosselen**	mussel
appel	apple	**nieren**	kidney
bonen	beans	**oesters**	oysters
boter	butter	**peer**	pear
eend	duck	**perzik**	peach
ei	egg	**pruim**	plum
garnalen	crab	**ree**	venison
ham	ham	**rijst**	rice
haring	herring	**rode wijn**	red wine
honing	honey	**rund**	beef
jam	jam	**rodekool**	red cabbage
kaas	cheese	**sinaasappel**	orange
kers	cherry	**snoek**	pike
kip	chicken	**taart**	flan
koek	cake	**varken**	pork
kool	cabbage	**wit brood**	white bread
kreeft	lobster	**witte wijn**	white wine
lam	lamb	**worst**	sausage
macaroni	noodle	**zalm**	salmon

INDEX

HANDY TRAVEL TIPS

An A–Z Summary of Practical Information

A

ACCOMMODATION (See also CAMPING, YOUTH HOSTELS, and the list of RECOMMENDED HOTELS starting on page 129)

The tourist offices in Bruges and Ghent are able to provide detailed lists of hotels in each city that describe facilities, prices, addresses, and phone and fax numbers. They can also book rooms for you on payment of a deposit, which is then deducted from your hotel bill. If you arrive in either city without a room, try this service first. In Bruges, contact Toerisme Brugge, Burg 11, B-8000, tel. (050) 44 86 86, fax (050) 44 86 00, or internet www.brugge.be/brugge. In Ghent, contact Dienst Toerisme van Gent, Botermarkt 17A, B-9000, tel. (09) 266 52 32 (the enquiry desk is in the crypt of the Stadhuis). Bruges is particularly busy in the summer months and at weekends, so it is advisable to book well in advance if you plan to visit at this time. If you are travelling in the low season or during the week, ask about discounts—many hotels do special deals from about October to March. The rates on page 129 are averages for double rooms in high season. Service charges and taxes are included. There is often a supplement for single rooms.

There is a star rating system (indicated in the tourist information literature and on a blue plaque by the front door of the hotel), but the number of stars bears little relation to what you may get. Some of the four-star hotels may have certain rated facilities but still be little more than dives, while hotels further down the scale can be delightful. A few hotel exteriors and foyers look splendid, but this can be deceptive. As always, it's best to inspect rooms if you can.

An extremely substantial breakfast is often included in the hotel rate. If you have to pay extra, do so, even if you're on a tight budget —it should be worth it, as you probably won't need lunch.

The Bruges tourist office also supplies a list of bed-and-breakfast accommodation in its brochure. A final alternative worth considering is staying as a guest in a private home under the Chambres d'Amis Benelux scheme. For further details about this service, contact Welcome Guest International, 27 rue Trixhe Nollet, B-4140 Dolembreux, tel. (041) 68 52 52, fax (041) 68 52 53.

What's the rate per night?   **Hoeveel kost het per nacht?**

AIRPORT *(luchthaven)*

For getting to and from Belgium, only Brussels National Airport at Zaventem is of any importance. It is served by many major airlines, including, of course, Sabena (Belgium's national airline), and has all the shopping and eating facilities you expect at an international airport. Although it is some 14 km (9 miles) from the centre of Brussels, there are bus, train, and taxi connections. The most convenient are the trains, which run every half hour to all three of Brussels' stations. The trip by taxi to the centre of town will cost you substantially more than by train, but a reduction in the taxi fare is available upon presentation of a round-trip air ticket. Special Sabena buses also connect the airport with Ghent.

   Luggage trolleys are available at the airport, and there are two numbers you can call for information on flight arrivals and departures: (09) 223 31 32 for Sabena and affiliated airlines, and (02) 732 31 11 for any other international airline.

B

BICYCLE HIRE/RENTAL

Bruges encourages cyclists by allowing them to travel down more than 50 one-way streets in either direction (not as dangerous as it sounds). Bikes can be hired or loaned from many sources. A growing number of hotels put bikes at their guests' disposal—ask when you arrive. They can be hired from the railway station in Bruges and Sint-Pietersstation in Ghent by the day. A discount is offered on presentation of a valid train ticket. In Ghent, tandems are also available. Bikes can be left at other participating rail stations—an information leaflet is available from stations and in advance from the Belgian tourist information office.

Other (more expensive) sources in Bruges are 't Koffieboontje at Hallestraat 4 (tel 33 80 27).

I'd like to hire a bicycle.   **Ik zou graag een fiets huren.**

BUDGETING for YOUR TRIP

Average, approximate prices in Belgian francs for basic items:

Airport transfer. Train from Brussels airport to Brussels Midi train station BF180.

Babysitters. BF200 per hour.

Bicycle hire. Generally from BF225–325 per day. At train stations BF150 per day on presentation of valid train ticket, BF335–650 (normal bikes) and BF615–840 (mountain bikes).

Buses. Ghent–Bruges one-day pass BF110.

Camcorder rental. BF1,000 per day. 60-minute tape costs BF519.

Camping. BF300–600 for a family of four for one night.

Car hire. BF2,000–2,500 for a small car.

Entertainment. Cinema BF220, ballet/opera tickets BF700–2,200, nightclub BF250 upwards.

Guides and tours. Qualified guide BF1,700 per 2 hours, BF850 per extra hour; boat trip BF160 (children half-price); horse-drawn cab ride BF800. Bruges: tourist office tour BF150 (children free); "Walkman" tour BF300; city bus tour BF380 (children BF250); Quasimodo's Fun Tours including picnic lunch and entrance fees BF1,400 (under 26 BF1,000); horse-drawn tram BF200 (children BF100); organized cycling tours BF450. Ghent: "Discover Ghent" tour BF780 (minimum 20 persons); powered boat hire BF1600 per 2 hours; organized pub crawl BF545–795.

Hotels. Expensive BF5,000+, medium BF2,500–5,000, inexpensive BF2,500 and below, for double room with bathroom and breakfast.

Bruges and Ghent

Meals and drinks (moderate). Breakfast BF200–250, lunch BF350, dinner BF600, coffee BF60, beer BF80–180, soft drink BF50.

Shopping. Belgian hand-made lace handkerchief BF400, Belgian chocolates per kilo BF500–1,000.

Taxi. Meter charge BF100 (BF180 at night), plus BF43 per km (75 at night).

Trams. Flat-rate price for Ghent trams BF40.

Trains. Brussels–Bruges BF760, Bruges–Ghent BF350, Ghent–Brussels BF470, Ghent–Oudenaarde BF240. Both ways.

Youth hostels. Bruges BF275–375, Ghent BF385–475, per person.

C

CAMPING

Belgium's campsites are graded from one to four stars and are usually excellently equipped. There are four recommended campsites in the vicinity of Bruges, which means you will have to find transport into the city centre. The tourist information office provides details and contact numbers for these campsites. Camping in Ghent seems largely confined to the four-star Blaarmeersen Sportcentrum and the one-star site at Witte Berken, details of which are also provided by the Ghent tourist office. The Belgian tourist office will provide a camping leaflet on request. It is advisable to book pitches in advance during the high season. Spending the night in cars, caravans, mobile homes, or tents by the side of the road, in woods, dunes, or directly on the beach is forbidden.

CAR HIRE/RENTAL (*autoverhuur*)
(See also DRIVING and BUDGETING FOR YOUR TRIP)

There are a lot of local car-hire firms in both cities, so if time permits you should compare prices. Both tourist information offices provide information on car hire, and firms can also be found in the yellow pages telephone directory (*gouden gids*). Credit cards are the preferred method of payment, and you will also need your driving licence and passport (but never leave them with the firm). Many hotels have arrangements with car-hire firms that make it simple to arrange for a car, but a small extra charge will normally be made for delivery to your hotel. The minimum age can be 20 or 25, depending on the company and the vehicle.

CLIMATE and CLOTHING

Belgium has a temperate climate much influenced by its proximity to the sea, although obviously this influence diminishes inland. The warmest and driest weather is between April and October, but it can rain at any time of the year. Approximate monthly temperatures in Bruges and Ghent are as follows:

	J	F	M	A	M	J	J	A	S	O	N	D
°C	5	6	10	13	19	21	23	22	20	14	8	6
°F	41	43	50	55	66	70	74	72	68	57	46	41

Clothing: The similarity to Britain's unpredictable climate means you should be prepared for rain at any time of the year. A raincoat is advisable, but many hotels provide complimentary umbrellas. In March and April, the weather can be bright and reasonably warm, but with sudden blasts of cold wind as you turn a corner—so a light coat that can be slipped on and off is a good idea. In winter, heavy coats and pullovers are advisable. Bruges and Ghent are walking cities, so take comfortable, reliable shoes that you know will not hurt, and take care over the cobbles.

Clothing is generally smartly relaxed and informal, but more expensive restaurants will expect male guests to wear ties.

Bruges and Ghent

COMMUNICATIONS
(See also OPENING HOURS and TIME DIFFERENCES)

Post offices (*posterijen*). The main post office in Bruges is at Markt 5. The main post office in Ghent is at Korenmarkt 16 (the interesting interior retains some original Art-Deco touches) and there is also one at Sint-Pietersstation. Opening times are 9am–5pm Monday–Friday, plus Saturday mornings. Smaller post offices close for lunch from noon until 2pm. Post boxes are red, often decorated with a white bugle. They are either free-standing or attached to walls. Stamps can also be purchased from souvenir shops and bookstores.

Faxes, telex, telegrams. Most hotels have fax and telex facilities; it is simplest to use these. Faxes and telegrams can also be sent during working hours from railway stations and post offices. Ghent has a telegram and telephone centre at 1 Keizer Karelstraat.

Telephone. The phone system run by Belgacom is reliable and extensive. Hotel phones are the most convenient, although they are expensive. Public phone booths are plentiful, particularly in the city centres and railway stations. The ones marked with European flags can be used to phone direct to most European countries, and have instructions in English, French, and German. Many booths accept phone cards rather than coins: cards can be purchased from post offices, bookshops, news-agents, and railway stations.

The telephone dialling code for Belgium is 32; Brussels is 02, Bruges is 050, and Ghent is 09. Belgium's telephone directory is known as the *gouden gids* (yellow pages).

A stamp for this letter/ postcard, please.	**Een postzegel voor deze brief/ briefkaart, alstublieft.**
airmail	**luchtpost**
registered	**aangetekend**

COMPLAINTS

If you have cause to complain, speak to the relevant person on the spot in the first instance, and then to the tourist information office or the police, depending on the nature of the complaint.

CRIME (See also EMERGENCIES and POLICE)

Its compactness and the numbers of tourists wandering its streets make Bruges extremely safe: You are seldom alone or far from the centre. There is very little crime, though obviously it makes sense to take elementary precautions with cameras, bags, and personal effects. Valuables should be left in your hotel safe.

Ghent, also, is very safe, but it is wise to stay clear of the small red light district between Keizer Karelstraat and Vlaanderenstraat, and the area around Sint-Pietersstation late at night. If plan on venturing far into outlying areas of either city late at night, your hotel receptionist should be able to advise you.

CUSTOMS and ENTRY FORMALITIES

Visitors from EU countries only need an identity card to enter Belgium. Citizens of most other countries including the US, Canada, Australia, and New Zealand must be in possession of a valid passport. European and North American residents are not subject to any health requirements. In case of doubt, check with Belgian representatives in your own country before departure.

As Belgium belongs to the European Union (EU), free exchange of non-duty-free goods for personal use is permitted between Belgium and the UK and Ireland. However, duty-free items are still subject to restrictions: Again, check before you go.

For residents of non-EU countries, restrictions when returning home are as follows: **Australia:** 250 cigarettes or 250*g* of tobacco; 1*l* alcohol; **Canada:** 200 cigarettes and 50 cigars and 400*g* tobacco; 4.5*l* wine or beer and 1.1*l* spirits: **South Africa:** 400 cigarettes and

Bruges and Ghent

50 cigars and 250g tobacco; 2l wine and 1l spirits; **US:** 200 cigarettes and 100 cigars or a "reasonable amount" of tobacco.

Currency restrictions. There is no limit on the amount of Belgian or foreign currency that can be brought into or taken out of the country by non-residents.

D

DRIVING (See also CAR HIRE)

To take your car into Belgium, you'll need:

- an international driving licence or your own driving licence (held for at least one year)
- car registration papers
- Green Card (an extension of your regular insurance policy, valid for travel abroad; though not obligatory for EU countries, it's still preferable to have it)
- a fire extinguisher and red warning triangle in case of breakdown
- a national identity sticker for your car

Driving conditions. Drive on the right, pass on the left. Though you may wish to drive to and from Bruges and Ghent, it is unnecessary and ill-advised to drive within the cities themselves. Bruges has a complex one-way system, with narrow winding roads that in high season are clogged with pedestrians and horse-drawn cabs. Driving in Ghent is more aggressive than in Bruges and is made more complicated by the presence of trams, which you are not allowed to overtake and to which you must give way.

Seat belts must be worn by both driver and passengers and there are stiff penalties for drunken driving. Some offences require payment of fines on the spot.

An important rule to remember is that drivers should normally yield to traffic approaching from the right. A yellow diamond-shaped sign with a white border indicates that drivers on main roads have the right of way. When the sign reappears with a diagonal line through it, then drivers must yield to traffic from the right.

Belgium's motorway system is superb, but it and the city ring-roads (like that in Bruges) can get clogged at rush hour. Other main roads in Flanders are generally very straight and free of traffic — weekday travelling is very good indeed. Belgium's accident record is, however, one of the worst in Europe.

Speed limits. On motorways, the limit is 120 km/h (75mph) and on other main roads it is 90 km/h (55 mph). In residential areas the speed limit drops to 60 km/h (37 mph).

Parking. There is limited parking in the city centres (mostly in the central squares). Tickets are purchased from machines on the pavement. Larger car and coach parks exist around the perimeter of Bruges; it's safer (and quicker) to use them and walk into the centre. Both tourist offices provide maps indicating car parks.

Breakdown. Belgium's two main motoring organizations are the TCB (Touring Club de Belgique) and the Royal Automobile Club de Belgique. They have reciprocal arrangements with other national motoring organizations and should be able to help you. Motorways have emergency phones positioned at regular intervals.

Fuel and oil. Service stations are plentiful, and most international brands of fuel are available. Four- and three-star unleaded (*loodvrij*) gasoline are sold, as are four-star leaded and diesel.

Road signs. International pictographs are in widespread use, but here are some written signs you may encounter:

Alle richtingen	All directions
Andere richtingen	Other directions
Beschadigd wegdek	Bad road surface
Eenrichtingverkeer	One-way street
Langzaam rijden	Slow

Bruges and Ghent

Moeilijke doorgang	Obstruction ahead
Opgelet!	Caution!
Tol	Toll
Wegomlegging	Diversion (detour)
Zachte berm	Soft shoulder

Are we on the right road for …? **Zijn wij op de juiste weg naar …?**

Fill the tank, please. **Vol, graag.**

Check the oil/tyres/battery. **Kijkt u even de olie/banden/accu na.**

I've broken down. **Ik heb autopech.**

Fluid measures

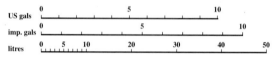

Distance

km	0	1	2	3	4	5	6	8	10	12	14	16
miles	0	½	1	1½	2	3	4	5	6	7	8	9	10

E

ELECTRIC CURRENT

Belgium operates on 220 volt, 50 Hz AC, requiring standard two-pin round continental plugs. Visitors should bring their own adapters.

EMBASSIES and CONSULATES *(ambassades; consulaten)*

Australia:	6 Guimardstraat, 1040 Brussels; tel. 231 05 00
Canada:	2 Tervurenlaan, 1040 Brussels; tel. 735 60 40
Ireland:	89 rue Froissant, 1040 Brussels; tel. 230 53 37

South Africa	(consulate): 26 rue de la Loi, 1040 Brussels; tel. 230 68 45
UK:	85 rue Arlon/Arlenstraat, 1000 Brussels; tel. 287 62 11
US:	27 boulevard du Régent/Regentlaan, Brussels; tel. 508 21 11

EMERGENCIES *(noodgeval)* (See also MEDICAL CARE and POLICE)

The three-digit emergency telephone numbers listed below are valid throughout Belgium:

Emergency/police	**101**
Accidents	**112**
Fire brigade/ambulance	**100**
I need a doctor/dentist.	**Ik heb een arts/tandarts nodig.**
hospital	**ziekenhuis**

ENVIRONMENTAL ISSUES

You may be tempted to buy exotic souvenirs, but spare a thought for endangered plants and animals that may be threatened by your purchase. Even trade in tourist souvenirs can threaten the most endangered species. So think twice before you buy—it may be illegal and your souvenirs could be confiscated by Customs on your return. For further information or a factsheet, contact the following:

UK: Department of the Environment; tel. (01179) 878000.

US: Fish and Wildlife Service; tel. (001) 703 358 2095; fax (001) 703 358 2281.

ETIQUETTE (See also TIPPING)

The citizens of Bruges and Ghent are open, friendly, and patient. Most will say that they speak only a little English, then go on to speak it fluently. It is courtesy to be polite and friendly in return. However, do not assume that everyone will speak English without asking first.

The great majority of bars, cafés, and restaurants permit smoking, often in designated areas.

G

GAY and LESBIAN TRAVELLERS

The national organization for gay men and women is based in Brussels at rue du Marché au Charbon 81, tel./fax 502 24 71; email ilga@glo.be. The age of consent for gay men is 16.

GUIDES and TOURS *(gids; tolk)* (See also MONEY MATTERS)

Bruges: Groups and individuals can book a qualified guide in advance from the tourist office, for a tour of minimum 2-hour duration. During July and August there are daily guided tours of the city, starting at 3pm from the tourist office. "Walkman" tours suitable for two people at a time are available from the tourist office.

Bruges's canals can be explored throughout the day, from 10am–6pm, though in winter on weekends and holidays only. Boats depart from Rozenhoedkaai, Dijver, and Mariastraat. Night tours for groups can also be arranged on request.

A 50-minute tour by bus with taped commentary in the language of your choice is operated by Sightseeing Line, with minibuses departing from the Markt at regular intervals. The same line operates tours to Damme for different durations, depending on the season: they also depart from the Markt and can include a free drink and pancake in Damme, and a return canal trip on the *Lamme Goedzak* paddle boat. Quasimodo's Fun Tours run a variety of minibus tours of the countryside and Flanders Field, offering a beer-themed itinerary.

Horse-drawn cab rides through the city centre depart from the Burg, with a 10-minute break for the horse at Minnewater. Commentary is provided by the driver. Horse-drawn trams depart daily from 't Zand for a 45-minute tour of the city.

Cycling tours in and around Bruges (following back roads) include provision of a mountain bike, guide, transport by bus, insurance, and rain gear; tel. (050) 34 30 45.

Ghent: The tourist office provides details of qualified guides for tours of minimum 2-hour duration. A "Discover Ghent" guide includes a qualified guide, boat excursion, and visit to the Belfort.

Guided tours (in various languages) by boat through the city-centre canals last 45 minutes: boats depart from Korenlei and Graslei. Scheduled boat trips to Bruges and Oidonk are also available in summer from Benelux Rederij, Recolletenlei 32, tel. (09) 225 15 05. You can hire four- and five-seater electrically powered boats: minimum age 16, book in advance—Rederij Minerva, Kareelstraat 6, tel. (09) 221 84 51. A group pub crawl involving a boat tour and walk with the town crier can be arranged: information and reservations from Orde van de Belleman, Rozemarijnstraat 23, tel. (09) 224 45 70.

From Easter through the end of October, every day from 10am–7pm, a 30-minute horse-drawn carriage ride through the city departs from Sint-Baafsplein.

L

LANGUAGE

About 60% of the population, roughly the northern half of Belgium, speaks Flemish (which is a dialect of Dutch). French is the language in Wallonia, southern Belgium, and a small percentage of the people in eastern districts speak German as their first language.

English is spoken and understood by virtually everybody. Both written and spoken Flemish are sometimes very similar to English; at other times there are no clues as to meaning. Menus may be printed in English as well as Flemish and French; if they are not, most staff will be happy to explain what things are.

Although local road signs are in Flemish, be aware that many towns bear different names in French. Brugge (Flemish) is *Bruges* in French; Gent/*Gand*; Ieper/*Ypres*; Oudenaarde/*Audenarde*.

Bruges and Ghent

Good evening	**Goedenavond**
Goodbye	**Tot ziens**
today	**vandaag**
yesterday/tomorrow	**gisteren/morgen**
day/week	**dag/week**
month/year	**maand/jaar**
left/right	**links/rechts**
good/bad	**goed/slecht**
cheap/expensive	**goedkoop/duur**
hot/cold	**warm/koud**

Days and Months

Monday	**Maandag**	Friday	**Vrijdag**
Tuesday	**Dinsdag**	Saturday	**Zaterdag**
Wednesday	**Woensdag**	Sunday	**Zondag**
Thursday	**Donderdag**		

January	**Januari**	July	**Juli**
February	**Februari**	August	**Augustus**
March	**Maart**	September	**September**
April	**April**	October	**Oktober**
May	**Mei**	November	**November**
June	**Juni**	December	**December**

Numbers

0	**nul**	12	**twaalf**
1	**een**	13	**dertien**
2	**twee**	14	**veertien**
3	**drie**	15	**vijftien**
4	**vier**	16	**zestien**
5	**vijf**	17	**zeventien**
6	**zes**	18	**achttien**
7	**zeven**	19	**negentien**
8	**acht**	20	**twintig**
9	**negen**	21	**een en twintig**
10	**tien**	30	**dertig**
11	**elf**	40	**veertig**

50	**vijftig**	80	**tachtigtig**
60	**zestig**	90	**negentig**
70	**zeventig**	100	**honderd**

LAUNDRY and DRY-CLEANING *(wasserij; stomerij)*

The large hotels offer same-day or next-day service, but not on weekends and holidays—and it's expensive. Dry cleaners and launderettes seem few and far between in both cities, but they will be cheaper. In Bruges, try the Press Shop at Nordzanstraat 5, which does dry-cleaning, washing, pressing, and minor repairs.

When will it be ready?	**Wanneer is het klaar?**
I must have it for tomorrow morning.	**Ik heb dit morgenvroeg nodig.**

LOST PROPERTY

It is best to first contact the police. In Bruges, the police station is at Hauwerstraat 7, tel. 44 88 44. In Ghent, contact the nearest police station, found under *Politie* in the phone book. Taxi drivers usually hand things to the police or to their head office.

I've lost my …	**Ik ben mijn … kwijt.**
handbag	**handtas**
passport	**paspoort**

MEDIA

Newspapers *(krant; tijdschrift)*. The best places to look for English-language publications are at the railway station kiosks and larger bookshops and news-agents. Larger hotels often stock the *International Herald Tribune* and *The Times*.

Radio and television. BBC long-wave and world services and European-based American networks can be picked up easily.

Bruges and Ghent

Most hotels have cable television with up to 30 channels, including both BBC channels and ITV from the UK, and CNN from the US. Many domestic and European channels show English-language films and imported programmes with subtitles.

Have you any English newspapers?   **Heeft u Engelse kranten?**

MEDICAL CARE (See also EMERGENCIES)

Travellers from EU countries should receive free medical treatment in Belgium. For citizens of the UK this means presenting an E111 form, which can be obtained from the post office—if you are still charged for treatment and drugs, you will have to seek reimbursement from the UK Department of Health. However, it is wise to take out extra travel insurance, which should cover illness, accident, and lost luggage. For non-EU citizens, travel insurance is essential.

Belgian pharmacies (*apotheek*) are identified by a green cross and should have a list in their windows of nearby late-night pharmacies. Such lists are also published in the local weekend press.

Where's the duty pharmacy? **Waar is de dienstdoende apotheek?**

MONEY MATTERS

Currency. The unit of currency in Belgium is the Belgian franc, abbreviated BF or FB. It is divided into 100 centimes (cts). Coins in circulation are: 50 cts, BF1, BF5, BF20, and BF50. Banknotes in circulation are: BF100, BF500, BF1,000, BF2,000, and BF10,000.

The Luxembourg franc, at parity with Belgian currency, circulates freely in Belgium and, though always accepted, is not very popular. Watch out for it in your change.

Exchange facilities. There is a standard commission for changing foreign currency and traveller's cheques. Generally, bureaux de change offer the best rates, followed by the banks. Hotels often exchange currency at an inferior rate. Currency-exchange machines at Brussels Airport make transactions in four currencies.

Credit cards (*credit card*). Major hotels and many restaurants and shops will accept payment by international credit cards.

Eurocheques are widely accepted throughout Belgium.

Traveller's cheques (*reischeque*) can only be cashed with passport identification belonging to the counter signature.

Sales tax, service charge. Called BTW, a sales (value-added) tax is imposed on most goods and services. In hotels and restaurants, this is always accompanied by a service charge. Both are included in the bill. For more expensive purchases there are special tax-free export schemes. Look out for shops displaying the signs Europe Tax-Free Shopping or Tax-Free International; retailers are well acquainted with the necessary procedures.

I want to change some pounds/dollars.	**Ik wil graag ponden/dollars wisselen.**
Do you accept traveller's cheques?	**Accepteert u reischeques?**
Can I pay with this credit card?	**Kan ik met deze credit card betalen?**

O

OPENING HOURS (See also PUBLIC HOLIDAYS, BRUGES MUSEUMS on page 32, and GHENT MUSEUMS on page 76)

Banks open Monday–Friday 9am–noon, 2–4pm. Some banks open on Saturday mornings and until 6pm on one or two days per week.

Museums are generally open all day from around 9:30am–5pm, but the smaller ones often close for an hour for lunch. In Bruges, they are closed on Tuesdays during the low season.

Post offices are open Monday to Friday 9am–noon, 2–5pm. Larger post offices are also open on Saturdays 9am–noon.

Bruges and Ghent

Shops and **department stores** are generally open Monday–Saturday 9am–5:30pm or 10am–6pm. Many smaller shops close for an hour for lunch. Late-night shopping on Fridays to 7pm. Closed on Sundays.

Important sights in Bruges: *Belfort-Hallen* Apr–Sep 9:30am–5pm, Oct–Mar 9:30am–12:30pm & 1:30–5pm; *Onze Lieve Vrouwkerk* Apr–Sep 10–11:30am & 2:30–5pm, Sat 10–11:30am & 2:30–4pm, Sun 2:30–5pm, Oct–Mar Mon–Fri 10–11:30am & 2:30–4:30pm, Sat 10–11:30am & 2:30–4pm, Sun 2:30–4:30pm; *Stadhuis* Apr–Sep 9:30am–5pm, Oct–Mar 9:30am–12:30pm & 2–5pm.

In Ghent: *Sint-Baafskathedral* 8:30am–6pm (except during services), *Ghent Altarpiece and Crypt* Apr–Oct Mon–Sat 9:30am–noon, & 2–6pm, Sun 1–6pm; Nov–Mar Mon–Sat 10:30am–noon & 2:30–6pm, Sun 2–5pm.

P

PHOTOGRAPHY and VIDEO

All makes of film and equipment are widely available, as is one-hour processing.

I'd like a film for this camera.	**Mag ik een film voor dit toestel.**
How long will it take to develop this film?	**Hoe lang duur het ontwikkelen van deze film?**

POLICE (See also Emergencies)

There are two sorts of police: the *rijkswacht*, responsible for crowd and traffic control, and the *politie*, responsible for general law and order. The *politie* are the ones you should approach if you need help, though both forces can be reached on the emergency 101 phone number. They are not that much in evidence on the streets (there is seldom any need for them), but they are usually dressed in dark blue. Any theft should be reported at the nearest police station.

Where's the nearest police station?	**War is het dichtsbijzijnd politiebureau?**

PUBLIC HOLIDAYS *(openbare feestdag)*

Most shops are closed on public holidays; if museums are not closed, they will be operating on Sunday hours. If a holiday falls on a Sunday, the following Monday will usually be taken off instead.

1 January	*Nieuwjaar*	New Year's Day
1 May	*Dag van de arbeid*	Labour Day
21 July	*Nationalefeestdag*	National Day
15 August	*Maria Hemelvaart*	Assumption
1 November	*Allerheiligen*	All Saints' Day
11 November	*Wapenstilstand*	Armistice Day
25 December	*Kerstdag*	Christmas Day
Movable dates:	*Paasmaandag*	Easter Monday
	Hemelvaartsdag	Ascension Day
	Pinkstermaandag	Whit Monday

R

RELIGION

Belgium is predominantly Roman Catholic, but Protestant Churches are also well represented. In Bruges, there is an English Church at Keersstraat 1 and an Ecumenical Chapel at Ezelstraat 83.

T

TIME DIFFERENCES

The following chart shows the time difference between Belgium and various cities in winter. Between April and September Belgian clocks are put forward one hour.

New York	London	**Belgium**	Jo'burg	Sydney	Auckland
6am	11am	**noon**	1pm	10pm	midnight

Bruges and Ghent

TIPPING

In a country where service is included in most bills, tipping is not a problem. Most people will not expect a tip. Possible exceptions are public toilets, where a tip of ten or so francs may be expected, and porter and maid service in the more expensive hotels.

TOURIST INFORMATION OFFICES

United Kingdom: Belgian Tourist Office, 29 Princes Street, London W1R 7RG; tel. 0891 887799, fax (0171) 629 04 54.

US: Belgian Tourist Office, 780 Third Avenue, Suite 1501, New York, NY 10017; tel. (212) 758 8130.

The information office in Bruges is in the Burg, tel. (050) 44 86 86, open daily 10am–1pm & 1:30–6pm during the summer, 9:30am–5:30pm in the winter. There is also one at the railway station, from where you can book hotel accommodation. In Ghent, the information office is in the crypt of the Stadhuis in Botermarkt, tel. (09) 266 52 32.

Where is the tourist office?   **Waar is het toeristen-bureau?**

TRANSPORT (See also MONEY MATTERS)

In cities where everything seems to be a short walk away, public transport is not usually a problem.

Buses: In Bruges, city buses to the suburbs can be caught most conveniently in the Markt or at the train station. Sightseeing buses and excursions also depart from the Markt. Other main bus stops are at Wollestraat, Biekorf, and Kuipersstraat. A one-day pass may be purchased, allowing unlimited travel on all the city's buses. Regional buses (to destinations outside Bruges) can be caught at the train station and in 't Zand. A free information help line is available for both types of bus at (059) 56 53 53, and schedules are also displayed in the tourist information office.

In Ghent, the main bus station is outside Sint-Pieters train station. This is also a terminus for many of the city's trams, which serve most of Ghent and are great fun to ride. Buses and trams can also be caught from the city centre outside the post office.

Trains: The Belgian railway network is superb. Bruges and Ghent are situated on the same line that connects Brussels with Zeebrugge. Train services are prompt and frequent. Announcements on inter-city trains are frequently given in Flemish, French, and English. Information and help are available at both cities' train stations.

The *B-Tourrail* ticket entitles the holder to 5 days' unrestricted travel for a period of one month anywhere in Belgium.

When is the next bus/train to ...?	**Wanneer vertrekt de volgende bus/trein naar …?**
I want a ticket to…	**Ik wil graag een kaartje naar…**
single (one way)	**enkele reis**
return (round-trip)	**retour**
first/second class	**eerste/tweede klas**

Taxis: Taxis are plentiful in Bruges and Ghent, where they flock together outside the train stations for the hotel run. Order your taxi at the hotel when you check out, and one will arrive in two or three minutes. They are rather more difficult to hail in the streets. In Bruges, you are most likely to find one in the Markt; in Ghent, outside the main post office.

TRAVELLERS with DISABILITIES

Facilities and accessibility to transport and buildings in both cities are distinctly patchy. The cobbled streets and medieval buildings of Bruges mean access to places of interest can be challenging, to say the least, particularly as ramps and railings are invariably absent. Some hotels have ramps, but planning rules for older hotel buildings forbid the installation of lifts, so all or some of the rooms can only be reached by the staircase. Museums are often similarly restricted, and may involve many stairs. The picture is much the same in Ghent.

Bruges and Ghent

Some of the larger (chain) hotels have specially designed rooms for guests with disabilities (see RECOMMENDED HOTELS on page 129). There are, at most, usually two or three such rooms per hotel.

No public transport seems to be equipped with lifts or ramps, and train carriages are frequently so high off the ground that one could do with a rope ladder.

At some major road crossings in both cities, textured soft paving has been installed. All travellers should be careful near the canals, which often are not railed off from the footpath or road.

Tourist information offices should be able to provide literature on those facilities that are available, and Bruges tourist information issues a map showing free parking facilities for drivers with disabilities.

In the US information for travellers with disabilities may be obtained from the Society for the Advancement of Travel for the Handicapped (SATH), 347 Fifth Avenue, Suite 610, New York, NY 10016; tel. (212) 447-7284, fax (212) 725-8253.

TRAVELLING to BRUGES and GHENT

By air: Brussels Airport (see AIRPORTS) is linked by direct flights with major airlines from all European and many North American cities, but other long-distance travellers may have to connect via Amsterdam, London, or Paris. There are no charter flights.

By coach: Many coaching holidays and direct coach services to Bruges and Ghent are available from European capitals (including London) and provincial cities.

By rail: Brussels, Bruges, and Ghent have excellent rail connections with the rest of the European network. There are various discount schemes: For non-EU residents, a Eurailpass allows unlimited first-class travel on most of Europe's railways except the UK's, while a Eurail Youthpass allows unlimited second-class travel for people under 26; EU residents can purchase an Inter-Rail or Inter-Rail 26+ card, valid for one month or 15 days; a Rail Europe S card entitles senior citizens to make reduced-price ticket purchases for European destinations (obtainable in Belgium before departure only); a Freedom Pass (available in the UK) allows travel on any 3, 5, or 10 days in a one-month period, for one particular country.

For people in the UK, the advent of the *Eurostar* service via the Channel Tunnel means travelling to Bruges and Ghent by rail has never been quicker and more convenient. Trains depart from Waterloo International (itself an architectural delight, with shops and cafés) and arrive in Brussels within 3½ hours: You can be in Bruges or Ghent in a bit over four hours. Check-in time is 20 minutes before departure, and your bags are with you at all times, so there is no delay waiting for luggage once you arrive. Any passport controls are at your final destination only. For first-class passengers, meals are served at the seat, while a buffet car is available for second-class passengers. The comfortable trains also have telephones. Seats should be booked in advance: This can be done direct or at some mainline stations and travel agents. There are also connecting and sleeper services from UK cities to London. If you do travel by *Eurostar* to Brussels and book your hotel through Belgian Tourist Reservations (tel. 32 2-513 74 84), you may qualify for discounted accommodation in Bruges and Ghent.

If you want to take your car, *Le Shuttle* travels between Folkestone and Calais every 15 minutes. Passengers stay with their car for the 35-minute journey.

By sea: A jetfoil (for pedestrians only) travels from London to Ostend and Ramsgate to Ostend. Ferry and hovercraft services depart from Dover, Ramsgate, and Felixstowe for Ostend and Zeebrugge, and from Hull to Zeebrugge. If you travel by Hoverspeed from Dover to Calais there is a direct bus from there to Bruges.

WATER

It is perfectly safe to drink tap-water in Belgium.

WEIGHTS and MEASURES

For fluid and distance see page 114. Belgium uses the metric system.

Bruges and Ghent

Length

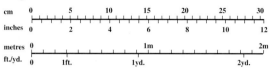

Weight

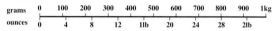

Temperature

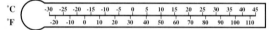

WOMEN TRAVELLERS

Women can wander anywhere in Bruges and Ghent without being subjected to sexual harassment. Avoid the red-light area of Ghent.

YOUTH HOSTELS

Bruges and its immediate neighbourhood has a number of "Youth Hotels" and Youth Hostels. The ones in the city itself are:

Bauhaus International Youth Hotel, Langestraat 135-137; tel. (050) 34 10 93, fax (050) 33 41 80.

The Passage, Dweersstraat 26, tel. (050) 34 02 32, fax (050) 34 01 40.

Jeugdverblijfcentrum VZW Snuffel, Ezelstraat 47-49; tel. (050) 33 31 33, fax (050) 33 32 50.

The attractive and well-equipped Youth Hostel in central Ghent is:

De Draecke, Sint-Widostraat 11 (Gravensteen); tel. (09) 233 7050, fax (09) 233 8001.

Recommended Hotels

With over 100 hotels throughout the city, Bruges presents more choice as to establishment and location, while Ghent's hotels tend to cluster in the city centre and around the station. Like everywhere else, hotels that are part of an international chain will provide a predictable degree of comfort, but guests may miss out on more authentic Flemish hospitality provided by locally-run establishments. Both tourist information offices provide brochures listing hotels.

It's always advisable to book in advance. Bruges is particularly crowded in the summer, tending to be busiest at weekends. Ghent is less crowded, but still busy.

Prices are based on the cost per night of a double room with *en suite* bath or shower, including service charge, VAT, and breakfast. Rates can vary according to the season or time of week.

❀	below BF2,500
❀❀	BF2,500–5,000
❀❀❀	above BF5,000

BRUGES

Acacia Hotel ❀❀ *Korte Zilverstraat 3A 8000 Bruges; Tel. (050) 34 44 11, fax (050) 33 88 17.* Centrally located in a reasonably quiet side street just off the Markt, this modern hotel (part of the Best Western chain) has 36 well-proportioned rooms, all with private bathroom, television, kitchenette, minibar, radio, telephone, and safe. Furnished in an inoffensive, international style, the hotel also has its own health club (with swimming pool), meeting rooms, and underground parking. The staff are friendly and welcoming. Major credit cards.

Alfa Dante Hotel ✹✹ *Coupure 29A 8000 Bruges; Tel. (050) 34 01 94, fax (050) 34 35 39.* About a ten-minute walk from the centre of Bruges, this quiet hotel is situated away from the crowds on the banks of a canal. The modern brick building has 22 rooms, all with bathroom, television, radio, telephone, and minibar. The atmosphere of the place is relaxed and friendly— staff are particularly helpful. The hotel has a small bar and conference facilities, and adjacent to the lobby in a conservatory there is an excellent vegetarian restaurant open to non-residents (see page 139). Major credit cards.

Azalea Hotel ✹✹ *Wulfhagestraat 43 8000 Bruges; Tel. (050) 33 14 78, fax (050) 33 97 00.* This is a comfortable family-run hotel in a 14th-century house on the banks of the Speelmansrei canal, 200 metres (250 yards) from the Markt. The 25 rooms (some in a new wing of the building) are furnished with bath or shower, radio, television, telephone, and minibar. There is a cocktail bar and terrace, and car parking is available. Some rooms are not accessible by lift—only by a lovely Art-Nouveau staircase. A family-home atmosphere prevails, with older but impeccable furnishings. Outside, the street can be busy until about 10pm, but then falls silent. Major credit cards.

Bourgoensch Hof ✹✹ *Wollestraat 39 8000 Bruges; Tel. (050) 33 16 45, fax (050) 34 63 78.* Superbly located at the junction of two canals, this quiet hotel is in a small square in the centre of the city. Most of the 11 spacious rooms are equipped with television and telephone. An excellent buffet breakfast is served in elegant surroundings, with festooned drapes, beautiful chandeliers, and luxuriant palms, and with views overlooking the canal. The hotel has a small bistro in the cellar and its attractive Flemish restaurant (also open to non-residents) is certainly worth visiting. Staff are more reserved than most, but still friendly and very helpful. Major credit cards.

Cavalier Hotel ✹ *Kuiperstraat 25 8000 Bruges; Tel. (050) 33 02 07, fax (050) 34 71 99.* A very small hotel of just eight rooms, all with bathroom, television, and telephone. A slightly ramshackle appearance from the outside conceals a friendly, ordered residence, if boasting rather bizarre murals, providing good value for the cheaper range of hotels. Dogs are allowed. Major credit cards.

De Orangerie ✹✹✹ *Kartuizerinnestraat 10 8000 Bruges; Tel. (050) 34 16 49, fax (050) 33 30 16.* This superb 17th-century residence on the banks of the canal opposite Dijver is ideally located, with lovely views from many rooms, each of which is individually furnished. The marble bathrooms are luxuriously equipped. Light spills in through the central conservatory onto paintings, antiques, and sofas. Breakfasts are served in a panelled dining hall with an enormous fireplace, or, on warm summer mornings, on the canal-side verandah. Guests are able to use the pool and sauna of De Tuilerieen, the sister hotel on the other bank of the canal. Staff are particularly friendly and helpful, even by Flemish standards. Unreservedly recommended. 19 rooms. Major credit cards.

De Tuilerieen ✹✹✹ *Dijver 7 8000 Bruges; Tel. (050) 34 36 91, fax (050) 34 04 00.* Sister hotel to De Orangerie across the canal, De Tuilerieen rivals its sibling in friendliness and comfort. Situated just a few doors away from the main museums, the hotel has 25 rooms, all with bathroom, television, telephone, and minibar. There is also a pool, sauna, and solarium, plus a small conference room, private bar, and car parking. The building, an elegant townhouse, is beautifully decorated throughout in creams, warm blues, and greens. Rooms to the front have fine views across the canal. An elegant place to stay. Highly recommended. Major credit cards.

Duc de Bourgogne ✹✹ *Huidenvettersplein 12 8000 Bruges; Tel. (050) 33 20 38, fax (050) 34 40 37.* Situated in the heart of the city in the historic Tanners Square, the Duc de Bourgogne is a small hotel of ten rooms occupying a most attractive step-gabled house overlooking the canals. Each room has its own bathroom and telephone, and the hotel as a whole is elegantly (perhaps rather heavily) furnished, with plenty of tapestries adorning the walls, chandeliers suspended from the ceilings, and brocade. The hotel restaurant has panoramic views along the canals of Bruges, but its Flemish cuisine can create a pervasive odour of fish in the hotel. Major credit cards.

Inter Hotel ✹ *Hoefijzerlaan 21 8000 Bruges; Tel. (050) 33 87 31, fax (050) 34 21 09.* In a fine Classical building, this hotel suffers slightly from its location on a very busy road, about ten minutes away from the city centre. The 13 rooms all have their own bathroom, television, and telephone, and there is a car park. Major credit cards.

Maraboe Hotel ✸✸ *Hoefijzerlaan 9 8000 Bruges; Tel. (050) 33 81 55, fax (050) 33 29 28.* An attractive, small hotel in a pleasant Classical building, but somewhat spoilt by the noisy road and underpass immediately outside. Pleasantly decorated in modern style in tones of orange and green, the nine rooms all have bathroom, radio, telephone, and television. There is also a small bar, and the hotel prides itself on its restaurant, which serves meals using ingredients brought fresh daily from the market. The hotel is just off the barren 't Zand square, ten minutes' walk from the city centre. Its rates, however, are at the low end of moderate, which makes it a comfortable place to stay for the money. Best ask for a room at the back. Major credit cards.

Novotel Brugge Zuid ✸✸ *Chartreuseweg 20 B-8200 Sint-Michiels, Bruges; Tel. (050) 40 21 40, fax (050) 40 21 41.* Situated in a southern suburb some 15 minutes' drive from the city centre, this hotel (part of the Novotel chain) is convenient for motorway connections to the rest of Belgium. Its 101 rooms (two for guests with disabilities) all have a television, telephone, and minibar. There is a comfortable bar and 24-hour dining room. This is a good hotel if you are travelling in a large group, or plan to tour around. Used a great deal by business people, the hotel has conference facilities and an outdoor swimming pool. The hotel's long corridors are dotted with shoe-polishing machines. Major credit cards.

Prinsenhof Hotel ✸✸ *Ontvangersstraat 9 8000, Bruges; Tel. (050) 34 26 90, fax (050) 34 23 21.* This is a family-run hotel in an extremely quiet location in the centre of Bruges, with its own car park. The elegantly furnished wood-panelled lobby sets the tone for the rest of the hotel, with its chandeliers, grandfather clock, and other antiques. Very comfortably furnished throughout in traditional style, the place has a warm, friendly atmosphere. Staff are helpful and friendly, and the rooms (with television, telephone, and minibar) are spotlessly clean, with marvellous bathrooms, gloriously fluffy towels, and complimentary toiletries. The breakfast is possibly the best and largest served in Bruges. One of the many accolades in the visitors' book summarizes thus: "A country-house hotel in the heart of the city." 216 rooms. Major credit cards.

Relais Oud Huis Amsterdam ✿✿✿ *Spiegelrei 3 8000 Bruges; Tel. (050) 34 18 10, fax (050) 33 88 91.* Situated on the picturesque Spiegelrei, this hotel is beautifully decorated in antique style. The tone is set by the lovely foyer staircase, climbing to 25 comfortable rooms, all of which have bathrooms, television, and telephone. There are views from the front rooms over the canal. The hotel has a bar and terrace, and there are also meeting facilities. Though there is a lift, the hotel is probably not suitable for people with disabilities. Major credit cards.

Ter Brughe ✿✿ *Oost-Gistelhof 2 8000 Bruges; Tel. (050) 34 03 24, fax (050) 33 88 73.* In a 16th-century house (unquestionably the most attractive hotel building in Bruges) in the elegant St. Giles quarter, this quiet hotel is five minutes' walk from the centre of Bruges. The Late-Gothic building was completely renovated in 1982 and now contains 24 rooms (some with lovely views over the canal), each with bathroom, television, and minibar. A substantial buffet breakfast is served in the 14th-century beamed and vaulted cellar, which once served as a warehouse for goods brought along the canal. The choice of furnishings sometimes seems at odds with the ambience of the building, and there is no lift, but it's a fine hotel nevertheless. Major credit cards.

GHENT

Alfa Flanders Hotel ✿✿✿ *Koning Albertlaan 121 B-9000 Ghent; Tel. (09) 222 60 65, fax (09) 220 16 05.* A few minutes north of the main railway station, this modern hotel has 49 bedrooms, each with bathroom, television, and telephone. The hotel also has a bar and a (rather dark) restaurant, plus car parking. The staff are friendly and courteous. Major credit cards.

Astoria ✿✿ *Achilles Musschestraat 39 9000 Ghent; Tel. (09) 222 84 13, fax (09) 220 47 87.* A 14-room hotel which adjoins the railway station and, as a result, is likely to be noisy throughout the night unless you ask for a room at the back. However, the proprietors have really made an effort to make the hotel comfortable. All rooms have their own bathroom, television, radio, and telephone. There is an attractively spacious breakfast room and the hotel has been comfortably decorated and furnished throughout. Private parking is at the rear of the neatly shuttered building. A worthy place to stay Major credit cards.

Chamade ✿✿ *Blankenbergestraat 2 9000 Ghent; Tel. (09) 220 15 15, fax (09) 221 97 66.* A comfortable modern hotel of 36 rooms just a few minutes north of the railway station. You feel here that a little effort and imagination have been used; for example, instead of sending guests downstairs to the bar and breakfast room, these rooms have been located on the top floor, thus making the most of a panoramic view across the city. Staff are extremely friendly and helpful, and the place has a cosy intimacy quite unusual in a modern hotel. The tastefully decorated rooms are spacious and equipped with bathroom, television, telephone, and a minibar, plus desk areas. There is a small conference room and some private parking. Special weekend and group rates are available. Major credit cards.

Flandria ✿ *Barrestraat 3 9000 Ghent, Tel. (09) 223 06 26, fax (09) 233 77 89.* An extremely cheap and basic hotel about a five-minute walk from the Botermarkt on a quiet side-street. The 21 rooms are very simply furnished. Some have no carpets, all are small, and only 13 have bathrooms. Generally clean, but you may encounter cracked handbasins and mysterious holes in the bath. A hotel where you sleep and wash and do nothing else, it is ideal for a very cheap overnight stay, and tends to accommodate younger guests on a shoestring budget. Breakfasts are substantial and the staff are very friendly. No deception involved—what you see is what you get. No American Express.

Gravensteen Hotel ✿✿ *Jan Breydelstraat 35 B-9000 Ghent; Tel. (09) 225 11 50, fax (09) 225 18 50.* Situated in a 19th-century mansion in a central location across the water from Gravensteen Castle, many of this hotel's 26 rooms have fine views over adjacent rooftops. This hotel projects itself as a luxury establishment, but once you get beyond the imposing entrance hall there lurks quite an ordinary hotel. The Gravensteen's rooms are equipped with bathroom, television, radio, telephone, and minibar, but the constraints of the old house mean that bathrooms are often cramped and squeezed into corners like afterthoughts. Breakfasts are not up to the usual Flemish standards. Under the same management as the St. Jorishof-Cour St. Georges (see page 136). Major credit cards.

Hotel Sofitel Gent-Belfort ✿✿✿ *Hoogpoort 63 B-9000 Ghent; Tel. (09) 233 33 31, fax (09) 233 11 02.* Probably the best hotel in Ghent, the Sofitel stands opposite the Stadhuis in a superb central location. Its 127 rooms are well-appointed and tastefully decorated in modern style, with splendid bathrooms, television, radio, and telephone. Public areas like the foyer and corridors are spacious, and there is wheelchair access. The restaurant serves a wonderful, delicious breakfast and traditional Flemish cuisine, as well as food from other countries on special occasions. Staff are friendly, discreet, and efficient. There are two comfortable bars (one of which is in a historic crypt), plus a fitness room and sauna, banqueting and seminar facilities, and car parking. Not as costly as many of the hotels in the "Expensive" category, the Sofitel provides fine value for money. Highly recommended. Major credit cards.

Ibis Gent Centrum Kathedraal ✿✿ *Limburgstraat 2 B-9000 Ghent; Tel. (09) 233 00 00, fax (09) 233 10 00.* Superbly located just across the road from Sint-Baafskathedraal, this modern hotel has 120 rooms, all with bathroom, television, and telephone, and striking blue floral bedspreads setting a cheerful tone. There is a restaurant, bar, and car park. Fine views of St. Baafsplein, the cathedral, and the Belfry can be had from many of the rooms in the front of the hotel, which are surprisingly quiet. There are also a small number of rooms designed for guests with disabilities. Staff are friendly. Another Ibis hotel, the Gent Centrum Opera, is at Nederkouter 24-6; Tel. (09) 225 07 07, fax (09) 223 59 07. Major credit cards.

Novotel Gent Centrum ❀❀ *Goudenleeuwplein 5 9000 Ghent; Tel. (09) 224 22 30, fax (09) 224 32 95.* One of the most attractive hotels in the Novotel chain, built around a central courtyard and located right in the middle of Ghent. The crypt incorporates 14th-century foundations, above which you will find a spacious reception foyer and comfortable bar. The 117 rooms are of the standard Novotel-type design, equipped with bathroom, a television, and telephone—the rooms that face the courtyard are particularly quiet. There are a few rooms designed for guests with disabilities. Breakfasts are substantial and of good quality. There is also a restaurant, swimming pool, meeting rooms, and car park. Major credit cards.

St. Jorishof-Cour St. Georges ❀❀ *Botermarkt 2 9000 Ghent; Tel. (09) 224 24 24, fax (09) 224 26 40.* Centrally located opposite the Stadhuis, this hotel, which is under the same management as Gravensteen Hotel, offers a small number of relatively comfortable rooms in its historic main building, plus basic motel-style accommodation in an annexe across the road. The main building dates back to 1228 and has rich historical associations. Note that while the hotel displays photographs of its best rooms, you may well be led to the annexe, where rooms are tastelessly decorated, cramped, and dark—many with no outlook at all. The lift is little more than shoulder-width. Breakfasts are served in the main building, but are poor affairs by Flemish standards. Most of the establishment's business revolves around its traditional and highly popular Flemish restaurant. 28 rooms. Major credit cards.

Trianon I ❀ *Sint-Denijslaan 203 9000 Ghent; Tel. (09) 221 39 44, fax (09) 220 49 50.* One of the hotels situated to the (noisier) south of the railway station, the Trianon II is about a five-minute tram ride from the city centre. The 19 rooms of this small modern hotel are perfectly acceptable and comfortable, making it a fine choice if you are on a tight budget. All rooms have their own bathroom and telephone, and there is wheelchair access. The hotel has a small car park and garage facilities. A sister hotel, the Trianon II, offers added whirlpool-bath comfort at Voskenlaan 34; tel. (09) 220 48 40, fax (09) 220 49 50. Major credit cards.

Recommended Restaurants

There are so many places to eat in Bruges and Ghent that it is unlikely you will ever go hungry. Most cuisine is Flemish, which means in practice a menu dominated by seafood, but there are plenty of other choices available. Except for the most expensive establishments, it is rarely necessary to book ahead, although at the height of the season it is wise to arrive early to be sure of a table. Tourist menus and other set menus at a fixed price are very common and are the best value for money. It is also often cheaper to eat at lunchtime than in the evening.

Opening hours vary depending on the nature of the place. Cafés and bars are usually open for most of the day, as are many informal restaurants. Other restaurants will open for two or three hours to serve lunch, and then close until the evening. Prices are for a three-course meal including tax but not drinks.

✸	below BF600
✸✸	BF600–BF1,000
✸✸✸	above BF1,000

BRUGES

De Belegde Boterham ✸ *Kleine Sint-Amandsstraat 5 8000 Bruges; Tel./fax (050) 34 91 31.* Delightful window displays featuring circles of home-made bread may tempt you into this small whole-food café and pâtisserie, though in the summer months it may also be the tables set outside in the evenings. The friendly proprietor prepares all the meals herself on the premises. The menu includes fresh Flemish sandwiches and salads, and cakes and pies. No credit cards.

Bruges and Ghent

Den Gouden Harynck ✾✾✾ *Groeninge 25 8000 Bruges; Tel. (050) 33 76 37, fax (050) 34 42 70.* An exceptionally fine restaurant in a charming brick-built house at the sign of the herring. Inside, tables are adorned with rich starched tablecloths, portraits stare at you enviously from the walls, and a fire may blaze in the grate. If there is such a thing as Nouvelle Flemish Cuisine, this is it: fresh ingredients carefully prepared and stylishly presented. Caviar is something of a house speciality and the restaurant has a superb wine list. Major credit cards.

De Stove ✾✾ *Klein Sint-Amandsstraat 4 8000 Bruges; Tel. (050) 33 78 35, fax (050) 33 79 32.* A small and intimate corner restaurant, simply decorated, and which looks charming at night when the place is candlelit. Specializing in Flemish dishes, with an emphasis on salads, fish, and steaks, it also serves wonderful *tiramisu*. Fixed menus start from around BF950. Major credit cards.

Het Dagelijks Brood ✾ *Philipstockstraat 21 8000 Bruges; Tel. (050) 33 60 50, fax (050) 33 67 66.* Fresh breads and cakes are on sale here, but go in for breakfast, lunch, or tea, and revel in the family atmosphere. The room is dominated by an enormous table at which most customers sit, beneath a beamed ceiling encased in canvas. Choose from a tempting range of enormous, open sandwiches and salads (with vegetarian options), and simple but ravishing Tuscan lunches (Italian quality in Flemish quantities), accompanied by Bruges Tarweiber beer. No credit cards.

Koffieboontje ✾ *Hallestraat 4 8000 Bruges; Tel. (050) 33 80 27, fax (050) 34 39 04.* Located in a hotel of the same name, this corner café-cum-restaurant just off the Markt is informal (you could say bordering on disorganized) and invariably crowded. It offers a vast range of snacks, Flemish dishes, and some vegetarian options, all of which are posted in the window. The clientele is usually the younger backpacking set, attracted no doubt by the extensive set menus, which offer excellent value for money. If you really must have a waffle, you can try one here in relative safety. Major credit cards.

Ristorante le due Venezie ❀❀ *Kleine Sint-Amandsstraat 2 8000 Bruges; Tel. (050) 33 23 26, no fax.* A popular trattoria that quickly crowds in the evenings, so arrive early. A vast menu serving everything Italian (including vegetarian options) means choosing is something of a problem. Though once decisions are reached, teams of cheerful Italian waiters will shout orders at one another across tables and wend their way through the crowded restaurant carrying huge plates of food. Wheelchair access. No American Express.

Spinola ❀❀❀ *Spinolarei 1 8000 Bruges; Tel. (050) 34 17 85, fax (050) 34 13 71.* Just off the picturesque Jan van Eyckplein, this beautifully furnished restaurant is a joy to eat in. The comfortable chairs are rich in brocade, and tapestries adorn the walls. The food is in a class to match the surroundings: Fish is a speciality, so try the mouth-watering scampi in garlic butter or the traditional grilled eel. The restaurant has an extensive and excellent wine list; remember to leave room for the exquisite *tarte tatin,* another house speciality. Major credit cards.

Toermalijn Restaurant ❀❀ *Coupure 29A 8000 Bruges; Tel. (050) 34 01 94, fax (050) 34 35 39.* A small vegetarian restaurant in the conservatory of the Alfa Dante hotel. Service is extremely relaxed, leaving you plenty of time to loaf between courses, but when it does arrive employees are helpful and courteous. Hearty bean soups, main courses of rice and braised vegetables with exotic salads, and puddings of fresh fruit are the sorts of things to expect. Open for lunch and dinner; it may be wise to book ahead for the evening. Major credit cards.

Trium Trattoria ❀ *Academiestraat 23 8000 Bruges; no Tel./fax.* For reasons best known to themselves, the proprietors of this Italian eatery chose to decorate the place with Greek busts; they nevertheless serve a vast range of pastas and sauces, salads, and pizzas. Food can be eaten on the premises—comprising a spacious scrubbed-pine room—or taken away. The beautiful dried pastas in the window will tempt you in, and once you've eaten you'll want to return. It's open all day until 8pm and there are vegetarian options. Major credit cards.

GHENT

Buddhasbelly ✸✸ *Hoogpoort 30 9000 Ghent; Tel. (09) 225 17 32.* A sparsely furnished vegetarian restaurant that caters mostly to a student clientele. The menu is limited but acceptable, particularly if you cannot venture far from the city centre. A trifle disorganized; gaggles of people tend to gather in the doorway or at one of the larger tables. Major credit cards.

Casa de Las Tapas ✸✸ *Cordowaniersstraat 41 9000 Ghent; Tel. (09) 225 18 89.* In what is fast becoming Patershol's restaurant alley, this Spanish restaurant does a thriving trade (at lunchtimes particularly) so it pays to arrive promptly. Here you can mix with diners from all walks of life, including elderly Spaniards with a lifetime of eating behind them, so the food must be good. A friendly and lively establishment where you can chew in time to vibrant flamenco music. Visa only.

Het Dagelijks Brood ✸ *Walpoortstraat 9 9000 Ghent; Tel. (09) 224 18 25, no fax.* A little way out from the city centre, near the university, this sister to the Bruges establishment of the same name is similarly decorated with scrubbed tables and simple whitewashed walls. To the rear is an extra room with a stuccoed ceiling and panelled walls which, at the time of writing, was to be extended into the conservatory for additional dining space. The multilingual menus offer a superb range of enormous open sandwiches and salads, cakes, and beverages, with vegetarian options. The service, like that at its sibling, is friendly and efficient. No credit cards.

Jan Breydel ❋❋❋ *Jan Breydelstraat 10 9000 Ghent; Tel. (09) 225 62 87.* As you explore the city you will find yourself passing this restaurant again and again, as it's on a prominent street corner on a popular walking route. Overlooking the tiny Appelbrug Parkje (really a very small garden square) and on the banks of the canal, the restaurant affords diners fine views as they tuck in to their meals. Fish dominates the menu, served in various combinations, and is often accompanied by champagne (if you so desire). A place of obvious restrained elegance, perfect for that last treat before departure. Major credit cards.

La Malcontenta ❋❋ *Haringsteeg 9 9000 Ghent; Tel. (09) 224 18 01, no fax.* This Patershol-district restaurant serves one of the most specific of specialities—cuisine from the Canary Islands. What this means in practice is plenty of fish and *paella,* so if you are seeking a radical alternative to Flemish fish dishes, you may be disappointed. Menus start from around the BF1000 mark. This is one of those establishments where "vegetarian" means a choice of fish dishes. No American Express.

Oranjerie (Patershol) ❋❋ *Cordowaniersstraat 8 9000 Ghent; Tel. (09) 224 10 08, fax (09) 233 54 61.* This is a most attractive restaurant, which really looks its best in the daytime. Metal spiral staircases and fittings in painted yellows and whites invite you in for closer inspection of the food, principally meat and fish dishes of the region. It's the sort of place where the staff can be heard talking and clattering in the kitchen, so you know there are plenty of people hard at work to make your meal a good one—you won't be disappointed. Major credit cards.

Panda ❋❋ *Oudburg 38 9000 Ghent; Tel. and fax (09) 225 07 86.* Situated at the end of a small arcade adjacent to a health-food shop of the same name, this restaurant serves fish, vegetarian, and whole-food dishes. While the food is good and the service friendly, the dining room itself is curiously adorned in plastic and aquatic blues and greens. Visa only.

Patiron ❀ *Sluizeken 30 9000 Ghent; Tel. (09) 233 45 87, fax (09) 233 50 70.* At the time of writing, the proprietor was seeking to expand into new premises, so if this delightful café has moved from its Patershol home, it is well worth making an effort to seek it out. Breads, cakes, and a selection of delicious and substantial quiches in tempting displays draw you into the simple whitewashed room of five or six tables. Everything is made on the premises, including some hearty soups and a wonderful *tiramisu*. The Patiron is open all day for snacks and meals, and the staff are friendly and helpful. Superb vegetarian options. No credit cards.

Raadskelder ❀ *Botermarkt 18 9000 Ghent; Tel. (09) 225 43 34, fax (09) 224 05 89.* In the vaulted cellar beneath the Belfort, this vast restaurant and bar has row upon row of tables and deserves to be more widely known for its historic location. It is often very quiet, which means diners can feel they're eating in a mausoleum; a place designed for crowds, it is best to eat here when there are plenty of people. The Raadskelder offers a host of regional and tourist menus, and its central location makes it ideal for lunchtime eating. At night, the ceiling lamps glow enticingly and make the place look even more medieval. Major credit cards.

St. Jorishof-Cour St. Georges ❀❀❀ *Botermarkt 2 9000 Ghent; Tel. (09) 224 24 24, fax (09) 224 26 40.* An attractive and popular traditional Flemish restaurant in the historic surroundings of the St. Jorishof building. Comprising a single large room with a gallery to the front, the restaurant always seems to be doing a roaring trade, so it would be wise to book in advance. Specialities include salmon in asparagus sauce, grilled turbot, salad of artichoke, and medallions of lamb. Many of the dishes have a supplement, so watch the menu carefully. The restaurant often has special events; the regular Sunday brunches are worth experiencing. Major credit cards.

't Klaverblad ✿✿✿ *Cordowaniersstraat 61 9000 Ghent; Tel. (09) 225 61 17.* While most of the neighbouring restaurants try to lure you with music, "themed cuisine," and moderate prices, 't Klaverblad is unashamedly gastronomic and expensive. Decorated and furnished in a minimalist style, the restaurant offers fish and meat dishes in the Flemish tradition (cooked by the propietor), accompanied by excellent wines. Definitely for serious eaters who appreciate good food, it is bound to expand and be more likely than most to change addresses—watch out for it. Major credit cards.

Unicorn ✿✿ *Sint-Michielsplein 14 9000 Ghent; Tel. (09) 233 79 95, no fax.* Turn up promptly if you wish to capture the coveted window seat in this small café-restaurant. Simply furnished, with images of unicorns on its walls, this friendly establishment serves a superb (and enormous) all-day breakfast, plus excellent meals and snacks. For vegetarians, the vegetable cous-cous is one of the unmissable highlights of Ghent. The kitchen is in full view, so you can see exactly what's going on, and the staff are thick on the ground for attentive, friendly service. Major credit cards.

Vier Tafels ✿✿ *Plotersgracht 6 9000 Ghent; Tel. (09) 225 05 25, fax (09) 224 18 51.* Located in one of the serpentine and secretive alleys of the burgeoning Patershol district, this restaurant originally started with just four tables, hence its name. Now considerably enlarged, it has an ambitious menu of dishes from around the world—everything from Sri Lankan curries to Mexican bean dishes, as well as vegetarian options. The food is mostly very good indeed. Warning: The spicy dishes really are spicy. Major credit cards.

ABOUT BERLITZ

In 1878 Professor Maximilian Berlitz had a revolutionary idea about making language learning accessible and enjoyable. One hundred and twenty years later these same principles are still successfully at work.

For language instruction, translation and interpretation services, cross-cultural training, study abroad programs, and an array of publishing products and additional services, visit any one of our more than 350 Berlitz Centers in over 40 countries.

Please consult your local telephone directory for the Berlitz Center nearest you or visit our web site at http://www.berlitz.com.

Helping the World Communicate